12.9+   14.95

4.95   First Ed

6.95

9.95

8.95

THE $20,000,000 HONEYMOON

THE
$20,000,000
HONEYMOON

Jackie And Ari's First Year

by

FRED SPARKS

Published by

BERNARD GEIS ASSOCIATES

Distributed by The World Publishing Company

CONTENTS

v

THE $20,000,000 HONEYMOON

A FEW WORDS FROM A
THUNDERSTRUCK REPORTER

Every once in a while there has been recorded, in the pages of history, a great romance between two people of wealth, power, or beauty that has captured the imagination of ordinary citizens everywhere and diverted them, for a moment at least, from their own humdrum struggle for survival. In times past it was Antony and Cleopatra, Napoleon and Josephine, Victoria and Albert. Earlier in this century it was Edward, King of England, who abdicated his throne for a Mrs. Simpson of Baltimore, for, as he said, "the woman I love."

Now there is another such romance captivating millions, a romance that, because it is a riddle, is perhaps more fascinating than the great ones of earlier times. It is the courtship and marriage of the the former First Lady of the United States, Jacqueline Bouvier Kennedy, and Aristotle Onassis, who is one of the richest men on earth.

No writer of fiction would have the gall to suggest to his publisher a novel based on events as unlikely as those actually attending the union of Jackie and Ari. Who could accept the fact that the society-born widow of a President of the United States would marry a swarthy, superficially unattractive financial Greek pirate old enough to be her father? And that she would live with him on the most sumptuous yacht in existence and appear to be having a corking good time?

Once again—truth is stranger than fiction. For all this has come to pass. The Beauty has married The Beast, who turns out to be one swell fellow, which is as it should be.

For this reporter, covering the romance, as I have since its inception, has been a radical departure from my usual assignments. For several decades I have been occupied by international troubles and political maneuverings. Now I find myself wearing no longer the traditionally soiled trench coat of the war correspondent, or the shiny black suit of the political reporter, but the double-breasted Savile Row fashion of those who keep watch on the Beautiful People, here and abroad.

Personally, I vastly prefer my new mission. Moneyed romance is a far more pleasant beat than any international trade conference or, perhaps, violent unrest among the nomadic tribes of Outer Mongolia. And, ah! those fringe benefits! Journalism would be a more delightful profession if all stories were covered while sipping champagne.

Whether one reports on hostile guerrillas in a jungle or on pampered society women in a boutique, there is no substitute for leg work. And so I have talked with the headwaiters, chambermaids, hairdressers, and interior decorators who have served Mrs. Onassis. I have also picked the memories of some of Jackie's intimate friends

—and intimate enemies. And, of course, I have read virtu-
ally everything that has been written, in four languages—
in books, periodicals, and newspapers—about the first year
of the marriage.

Jackie, of course, needs no introduction. She is as well
known a legend as any American woman in history. But
Mr. Onassis' background is somewhat shadowy, to say
the least. And so I spoke to scores of people who have
worked closely with Mr. Onassis through the years, even
some who knew him when he didn't have a million to
his name.

I thought, as I pieced together his biography, that his
claim to fame is best illustrated in the story of the American tourist, who, on passing Ari in the streets of Monte
Carlo, said to her husband: "Why, Mr. Onassis is just a
little man!" Her husband replied: "Not when he stands
on his money!"

Because Jackie and Ari, since their marriage, have been
shuttling between America and Europe like a pair of
Pan American pilots, it has been essential for me, in order
to log their activities fully, to call on others for assistance.
To calculate the prodigious sums of money Mr. Onassis is
spending on the woman he loves, I had a helping hand
from a respected accountant in New York whose firm has
representatives in every commercial center. (As we delved
deeper into Mr. Onassis' personal expenses, the accountant, usually a taciturn man, became agitated and one day
he cried out: "Why, I do believe that Mr. Onassis' bills
would stagger the World Bank!")

To record Ari's and Jackie's movements in Greece, I
was fortunate in obtaining the services of the energetic
Costas Skouras, who is on the staff of *Vima*, a leading daily
in Athens. Mr. Skouras did everything but stow away

aboard the Onassis yacht, *Christina,* to keep a day-by-day diary. Tracking Jackie through the fashion (and cosmetic) salons of Paris and Rome on my behalf were two women, well-known experts in such matters, who must, for obvious reasons, remain anonymous. Reporting to me on the business deals of Aristotle Onassis and the other Golden Greek shipping men (and on their Golden Women) was the erudite Stephanos Zotos. Besides being the author of numerous scholarly books on ancient and modern Greece, Mr. Zotos, as an international journalist, has been writing about Ari for thirty years. The brilliant writer Liz Smith, friend of the Burtons and people like that, made some of her articles, books and notes available to me. And keeping me reasonably accurate about many subjects, including the fashion game, was journalist Albert McGuire of the Publishers-Hall Syndicate.

Without the above-mentioned aides, to whom I am warmly grateful, I would have been swamped in the details of this global romance, this bejeweled marriage. It is not easy to keep track of Jackie and Ari as they spend, as they are now doing, $1,500,000 a month.

PART ONE

From Camelot
To Jet Set

Chapter One

WHITE HOUSE HOLIDAY

In his bachelor days in the 1950's, as a Congressman, then as a Senator, John Fitzgerald Kennedy met Aristotle Onassis several times at dinner parties and receptions in New York and Washington. At that time Mr. Onassis, involved in complicated deals and litigation, was spending more time than usual in the United States, cultivating well-placed persons in the Truman and, later, in the Eisenhower administrations.

But the rising young politician from New England and the Greek, who was really a man without a country, never exchanged more than a few informal words, the kind one exchanges with a stranger at a cocktail party. Neither one, at the time, fitted in the other's scheme of things.

Jackie Kennedy herself had never met the modern Argonaut, but she had heard some mind-blowing **stories** about Ari from her sister, Lee. Lee and her husband, Prince Stanislas Radziwill, had a little house in a London mews where they often hosted the jet set. Several times Lee and her husband, "Stash," had been invited to sail on Onassis' superyacht, *Christina*. ("An invitation to cruise on the *Christina*," said one ancient playboy, "is as cherished a kudo for a member of the jet set as a cockney and his wife getting invited to take potluck with Elizabeth and Philip at the Palace—'just the four of us, luv.'")

In the summer of 1958, Senator and Mrs. Kennedy were house guests of his father, Joseph P. Kennedy, who had leased, for the mild months, a villa in the south of France. Onassis was aboard the *Christina*, riding at anchor in the harbor of nearby Monte Carlo, and *his* house guest was the former British Prime Minister, Sir Winston Churchill. Onassis heard that John Kennedy, who was then being ballyhooed for the Democratic Party's Presidential nomination, two years hence, was in residence not far up the Côte d'Azur. The day before, his wife, Tina (they were still married), had asked a couple of dozen Beautiful People to drop in for some light goodies and bubbly, and now Mr. Onassis dispatched a courier with an invitation to the younger Kennedys to join the party, and John F. accepted. The Senator had met Mr. Churchill when his father was the United States Ambassador to the Court of St. James. And Jackie had met the the old warrior the summer after her freshman year at Vassar when she had done the grand tour with two socialite pals. In London they had wangled invitations to a garden party given by Queen Elizabeth, and there had cornered Churchill and chatted with him.

When Onassis told Sir Winston that the son of Joseph P. Kennedy was coming, Churchill was pleased. Of course, he did not remember Jackie or the young man, who had been but one of the American Ambassador's sprawling contingent of children, but he did remember Joseph P. Kennedy, and not with any great enthusiasm. "Shortsighted ass" was one of his milder descriptions of the diplomat in question.

Sir Winston's distaste was based on Joseph Kennedy's close friendship with Mr. Churchill's predecessor, Neville Chamberlain, the umbrella man, and Joseph Kennedy's openly expressed belief that old England had had it and was doomed to be knocked down by Hitler's *Luftwaffe*, then stomped into submission by the *Wehrmacht*. Furthermore, Mr. Kennedy had made it quite plain that if the United States had any brains it would stay out of the war. But Sir Winston, who had led the fight against the Germans, and who had, almost as much as the bombing of Pearl Harbor, nudged America into the war, was no man to hold a grudge against the offspring of a man who was not one of his favorite people.

Mr. Onassis arranged things so that the Senator and Mr. Churchill could chat together in a quiet corner of the deck. Mr. Churchill, straightaway, asked the Senator what his chances in the next Presidential election were. The Senator, listing some of the barriers between him and the White House, said: "I am a Catholic, you know." Sir Winston replied: "If that's the only difficulty, you can change your religion and still remain a good Christian."

While Sir Winston talked politics with John Kennedy, Mr. Onassis, ignoring his other guests, gave Jackie a personally conducted tour of the *Christina*. A woman who dotes on sybaritic trappings, she was awed by the rich fixtures, and by the deep knowledge her host had of every objet d'art. Who could foresee, that, in the years ahead, this luxury craft was to be Jackie Kennedy's primary home?

Incidentally, the Kennedys left the party only minutes before the arrival of Maria Callas, the Italian opera star who, for nine years, was Ari's constant companion—almost to the day he married Jacqueline Kennedy.

A month later, when the Senator and his wife were back in Washington, Mr. Onassis sent to John Kennedy an excellently detailed bronze model of a whaling ship he had once owned. Senator Kennedy was delighted. Today the model, polished to a sheen, is prominently displayed in the living room of the apartment Jackie occupies with Aristotle Onassis on Fifth Avenue in New York.

The next five years were hectic ones for the young Kennedys: the race for the Presidency, the successful election, and then the honors—and tensions—of the White House itself. Mr. Onassis was seldom, if ever, a topic of conversation between Jackie and JFK. But during the early months of 1963 there was a lot of gossip kicked around Washington—and in the international jet set—to the effect that Lee Radziwill had practically become a member of the majestic *Christina's* crew, and that she was going to give her husband, the Prince, the deep six and marry Mr. Onassis.

The President and his brothers, Edward and Robert, didn't think much of this. An Onassis in the family, even by marriage to a sister-in-law, was *not* to be desired. The President and his brothers were well aware that Mr. Onassis was, to say the least, political dynamite. Besides Ari's often controversial business practices, his private life, in which he was associated with many of the most glamorous women on earth, was too far out, at least from the viewpoint of the politically minded Kennedys.

The President wondered out loud one night if Lee had flipped her lid. And Bobby, it is understood, went directly to Jackie and asked her to get in touch with her sister and tell her to drop Onassis. Now, this was just the sort of thing Jackie was not about to do. Lee's business was Lee's business, not Bobby's.

But the whole to-do about Lee and Ari was forgotten in the early fall when Jackie's two-day-old son, Patrick, died in a Boston children's hospital. When Jackie returned to the White House after that tragedy, she was very melancholy and nothing could snap her out of it. The President was seriously worried about her state of mind, for Jackie spent most of the time in her own suite, and refused to see almost everybody.

Then one day, out of the blue, she received an invitation, on heavily engraved note paper, from Aristotle Onassis inviting her to joint her sister, Lee, and some other friends on a lazy cruise of the Aegean Islands. (The invitation, as it turned out, was inspired by Lee.)

Jackie jumped with joy, although she sensed a battle royal ahead. But this was just the kind of rejuvenating vacation she needed. Delicious privacy away from the cloying pressures of official Washington! Glorious escapism!

The Onassis invitation for Jackie to cruise on the *Christina* began one of the most vocal and extended arguments John F. Kennedy and his wife ever had. It was so bitter, and at times even shrill, that it quickly became common knowledge among the White House staff, who are not above cocking an ear now and then.

Recalling the event, Lucianne Cummings, one of President Kennedy's speech writers, told me: "Those of us in the White House during the Kennedy years were quite

aware that, like so many other couples, the President and
Mrs. Kennedy had their differences. Indeed, there were
some very stormy periods, due to Jackie's insistence on
leading her own life even if it meant ignoring her husband's political obligations. The President felt that nothing
should ever interfere with *our careers*, as he put it. Every
time the President said this, Jackie would reply: 'I never
ran for office and never will, so come off it, John.'

"In any case, their two different points of view met head
on most severely over the Onassis cruise affair."

When Jackie produced the invitation and said she was
eager to accept it, the President and Bobby responded as
if she had requested permission to work nude in an off-
Broadway show. The Presidential press secretary, Pierre
Salinger, was sent for. His department had just managed
to calm down several columnists who had been ragging
Jackie, rather brutally, about her lavish purchases of expensive clothes. Now this!

While Bobby was for meeting the issue head on, the
President, although he dreaded the rocky newspaper treatment ahead, was also conscious of Jackie's recent depression. He wavered, then entirely ceased his opposition to
the cruise when Jackie assured him that, while Mr.
Onassis was placing his yacht and full crew at her disposal,
he would not himself be aboard. To make it official,
Pamela Turnure, the First Lady's Press Secretary, called in
the White House newspaperwomen and announced Mrs.
Kennedy's trip. And Miss Turnure made it very clear that
Mr. Onassis would not be on the passenger list.

For the occasion, the *Christina* had aboard a dance
band, and two coiffeurs to tend the female guests, who
included Lee and Mrs. Franklin D. Roosevelt, Jr. The
yacht sailed from Piraeus and made several stops, con-

stantly shadowed by the press. No Mr. Onassis. But when
it docked in Istanbul, to the amazement of waiting reporters, down the gangplank came Mr. Onassis, who had
obviously remained hidden at the previous ports of call.
Later it leaked out, at least in White House circles, that
Mr. Onassis had been talked into touring Turkey with his
guests by none other than the ever-independent Jackie
Kennedy, who, as one observer put it, "got sick and
tired of the silly, uncalled-for secrecy." Here again, Jackie
was asserting her intention to live her own life. The
news of the small deception caused an uproar. The Greek
press, at least that part of it hostile to the shipowner,
chided Mrs. Kennedy for dignifying Onassis by her presence. And in Washington, Congressman Oliver Bolton of
Ohio said it was disgraceful that the First Lady should
accept the hospitality of a man who had been indicted by
and was in heavy debt to the U.S. Government, and was,
generally, a person of unsavory reputation. "If Mr. Onassis
were an American shipowner," said Congressman Bolton,
"a clear conflict-of-interest question would be raised."

On top of that the columnists, who pounced on the
story, said that the real reason Onassis had invited Mrs.
Kennedy was to upstage his rival shipping tycoon, Stavros
Niarchos, who had recently been host, on *his* yacht, to
Princess Margaret.

"The President," Lucianne Cummings recalls, "simply
exploded. Using the special microwave hookup that had
been arranged, at considerable cost, between the White
House and the *Christina,* the President called Jackie and
said: 'I know you're on the high seas, and I don't care
how you get off that yacht, but *get off!* Jackie, you're a
good swimmer.'"

The *Christina* sailed on, with Jackie *and* Ari very much

aboard. There was nothing to indicate that Mrs. Kennedy cut her cruise short by one hour; independence was her life style. The President of the United States, who had managed, in an eyeball-to-eyeball confrontation, to get Soviet missiles off Cuba, now seemed totally unable to get his wife off Aristotle Onassis' yacht.

The White House staff was abuzz with this unprecedented defiance. One secretary gasped: "Why, Jackie has seceded from the Union!" Another remarked: "The only thing the President can do now is to send the Mediterranean Tactical Marine Force to board the *Christina* and remove Jackie in irons."

Meanwhile, Jackie was having a high time. With Ari she went down the *Christina*'s Jacob's ladder to board a bobbing small craft and skim along close to the legendary island of Lesbos. To inspect the Palace of Minos, Jackie was accompanied by Onassis, one Secret Service man, and two women. At the palace itself, reported the United Press, she was fascinated by "the Queen's apartment, where she admired the ruins of the ancient boudoir, bedroom and vials in which the Queen used to keep her perfume."

The President received Jackie, when she returned to Washington, with less than his usual enthusiasm, according to Miss Cummings. And the pleasure of having her company again was yet more diminished when she showed him a small fortune in jewels—bracelets, pins, rings—from the jeweler Zolotas in Athens that Mr. Onassis had pressed upon her as souvenirs of his beloved Greece. (What an avalanche of jewels would follow in the years to come!)

"Nothing remains secret very long in the glass house that is the Presidential mansion," said Miss Cummings, "and it wasn't long before those of us who ate in the

White House mess were talking about Mr. Onassis' gifts, and we all knew that the President, in an unguarded moment, with servants within earshot, had blurted out, with deep sarcasm: 'All I need now is for Congressman Bolton and Drew Pearson to get wind of this. If they do, Jackie, you can start looking for a new place for us to live in after January 20, 1965.' "

Lee Radziwill, perhaps without malice, rubbed more salt in the President's wounded vanity when she wrote him a letter, from her home outside London, in mock complaint "that while Jackie has been laden with presents I only received three dinky little bracelets that Caroline wouldn't wear to her own birthday party."

Jacqueline Kennedy was never again the same woman. The cruise with Onassis had been a turning point in her life. Jackie, who had thought she had seen everything in the world, had never before seen such a luxurious, easygoing manner of living. She had been delighted with living on a floating palace, and getting up every morning without a care in the world, without even a letter to sign. Now every day in the White House she again had to face at least one disagreeable chore. Perhaps she had to meet with, and be pleasant to, a committee of battle-axes, say the Petunia Lovers of Philadelphia. Or to show around the Executive Mansion a gaggle of Midwestern school children, clutching peanut butter sandwiches and demanding, every other minute, to use the convenience.

Life on the *Christina* was entirely devoid of routine, and the grubby things of life were abolished, as if by royal decree. Each morning Mr. Onassis had let her decide in what direction the yacht would go, what port to visit.

Mrs. Kennedy was also immensely impressed by Mr.

THE $20,000,000 HONEYMOON

Onassis, and she told everybody just that. While she had known men of great wealth and great power before, she had never known anyone who handled these assets with more ease. "Onassis is no more conscious of his wealth," said Jackie, "than Rock Hudson is conscious of his good looks. It just comes natural to them—even though Rock was born with his blessings, while Ari had to work like a galley slave to get his."

Lucianne Cummings remembers that "on Jackie's return from her cruise with Onassis she seemed detached, ethereal. One of the girls on the White House staff observed: 'Jackie has stars in her eyes—Greek stars.'"

At the time, Mary Barelli Gallagher, Jackie's private secretary, made this observation: "I recall that when she got back she asked me to record Onassis' winter address in my address book—on Avenue Foch in Paris (where he lived with Maria Callas) and also his address in Athens, on Vasileous Georgiou—Glyfada. I mailed a letter to his Athens address. . . .

"Among my bits and pieces of notes to myself from White House days, I see one dated 10/18/63 that says: 'Big cigarette box—Mr. Onassis.' . . . Knowing how important lovely cigarette boxes were to Jackie, I assume that she gave a cigarette box as a thank-you note to Onassis."

Was there, during the cruise, or at any time afterward, a sense of rivalry between Jackie and Lee concerning Mr. Onassis? Did Jackie, as some of the more hysterical fan magazines have said, "push Lee aside"? There is no evidence to support such charges. Without doubt, the relationship between Lee and Ari had been blown up out of all proportion; Lee is still very happily married to the Prince. And certainly Lee and Jackie have been, if anything, closer than ever since that cruise.

On November 22, 1963, slightly more than one month after Jackie Kennedy concluded her cruise with Onassis, John Fitzgerald Kennedy was shot at her side.

The day before, on November 21, Aristotle Onassis bid farewell to Maria Callas in their villa outside Athens and flew to Hamburg. November 22 was a red-letter day for Ari. One of his tankers, the thoroughly modern 50,000-ton *Olympic Chivalry*, was launched at a gala champagne-smashing ceremony while a uniformed, old-fashioned German band went *oompah, oompah, oompah*. That night a vast feast of celebration had been laid on. When Mr. Onassis arrived at the restaurant the *maître d'*, his face in torment, said: "Herr Onassis, I just heard it on the radio, someone has shot President Kennedy!"

Mr. Onassis went through the dinner and the endless toasts and speeches, like a man walking in his sleep. The following day, after much soul-searching, he phoned Maria Callas in Athens and told her he would not be coming back, as originally planned, directly to Greece. Then Ari boarded an airplane for New York, where he transferred to another one for Washington.

It was noted by the press that Mr. Onassis was one of the few nonofficial, nonfamily acquaintances to pay his respects to Mrs. Kennedy in her private suite in the White House after her husband's state funeral.

Chapter Two

THE NEW JACKIE

For almost two years after President Kennedy died, Jacqueline Kennedy was practically a recluse. She seldom went out, and received few visitors except members of her own family or the Kennedy clan. One of the few outsiders who regularly called on her was Aristotle Onassis.

At the time, Jackie and the children were staying in a town house in the Georgetown section of Washington, and Mr. Onassis' visits were always welcome. For one thing, he brought valuable gifts for everybody—Caroline started calling him "Santa Claus." One time in 1964 Ari brought Jackie a stunning cigarette case from Van Cleef & Arpels, which she cherished. Another time he brought her an antique Dutch music box, which she played over and over again in her bedroom.

But more than bringing gifts, Ari brought with him a vast number of amusing anecdotes, and he collects anecdotes as lovingly as he collects money. He thought Jackie was taking herself too seriously, and one night he told her so. "Jackie, you have no right to isolate yourself like this," said Mr. Onassis. "It is not good for you, and not good for the children. You have done all the mourning that anyone can humanly expect of you. The dead are dead. You are the living. Come on, Jackie! Rejoin the world! I'm sure that is what the President would have wanted."

In this approach Mr. Onassis was different from most of her other visitors. They seemed to regard her as a public shrine. The Kennedy admirers seemed to think she should wear widow's weeds forever. It seemed incredible, but they expected Jackie, a woman in the full richness of her life, to spend the rest of her days in solemn contemplation of her terrible loss, to go into a permanent decline the way Queen Victoria had done after her consort, Albert, died.

One particularly important statesman (according to one of Jackie's secretaries) came for dinner one night, a full fourteen months after the President was killed. Throughout the entire evening he harped on one subject: the great, irreplaceable loss the nation had suffered. He went on and on with this theme. It was like a funeral oration. By the time he left, Jackie was in tears and needed a tranquilizer.

"For God's sake," she sobbed, "the way the man talked you'd think I never even existed. What am I supposed to do? Perhaps the best thing is if I had been buried along with Jack, at least that's the way *they* feel. Maybe we should import to this country the Indian custom of women throwing themselves on the funeral pyres of their husbands."

One thing is sure, Jackie gave Mr. Onassis' words months of deep thought. Perhaps it was at this point that she began her still-growing hostility toward the Kennedy clan. Although Bobby and Teddy never came out and said so, it was very obvious that they wished her to continue her role of grief-stricken widow.

Finally, in 1965, Mr. Onassis convinced her that the only way to start a new life was to get away from Washington, with all its awful memories. And so Jackie startled her staff by announcing that she had bought a fifteen-room apartment—a $200,000 co-op—at Fifth Avenue and 85th Street in New York. She moved out of Washington, bag and baggage. She even discharged most of her secretarial and domestic staff. She wanted to make a clean break.

In New York, Jackie was reborn almost overnight. She dispensed with the somber gowns of mourning. She again became a familiar sight in the smart dress shops and restaurants. She looked and acted ten years younger and everybody was delighted—except those who had sought to make political capital out of her role as the national widow.

Gradually, as the months went by, as Jackie fully emerged from her uncharacteristic cocoon, as she dropped a lot of the old Washington hangers-on, some critics began to say that *this* was the real Jackie. The real Jackie whose heart belonged to the world of fashion, the arts, the theater, and even to the jet set. Now the "experts" were suddenly saying that Jackie never really did belong to the Kennedy world of continual politics and family togetherness. And for once they were right.

In almost no time at all, Jackie became accepted, in the smart East Side region she patronizes—east of Central Park from 50th Street to 86th Street—as something of a swinger, with, of course, many reservations. For instance, the first party she gave after the long traumatic months of being closeted in relative isolation was, to put it mildly, a blast.

First, she had to have a guest of honor (a party needs a reason), and she selected her late husband's friend, John Kenneth Galbraith, the economist, whom President Kennedy had appointed Ambassador to India. Perhaps one reason the Chief Executive rewarded him for political services rendered was to keep him as far removed as possible from Washington, where his unorthodox language shocked the cliff-dwellers of capital society. (Reporting to the President on one occasion about the lack of security shown in the delivery of American arms to India, Galbraith wrote: "A few weeks ago one of our aircraft carriers brought twelve supersonic jets to Karachi, where they were unloaded with all the secrecy that would attend mass sodomy on the BMT at rush hour.")

Having selected the controversial Professor Galbraith as her guest of honor, Mrs. Kennedy then invited a hundred of the most diverse characters from New York, Washington, Newport, and Palm Beach to the Sign of the Dove. Jackie's guest list included some citizens who could trace their families back to the Pilgrims, and others who could trace their families back to Leavenworth Penitentiary.

Among those invited by the former First Lady was pop artist and underground moviemaker Andy Warhol. Andy arrived accompanied by his "movie star," Edie Sedgwick, who was not recognized even by those present who had seen all her movies. Miss Sedgwick came to the Sign of the Dove dressed.

Andy wore his usual stunning attire: camp, camp, camp. Besides his yellow-tinted outsized eyeglasses, he had on his leather jacket, and his black pants, so tight they looked like a coat of paint.

To keep her guests jumping, Jackie had hired Killer Joe Piro, then one of the leaders of the rock 'n' roll scene. The amplified music was so loud that one Newport matron, an ardent supporter, in her day, of Calvin Coolidge, told her companion, as she took off her hearing aid: "For the first time in a decade I can hear the music without this contraption."

Jackie herself was radiant that night, a night that could well be described as her second coming-out party. (At her first, in Newport's Country Club, the likes of Andy Warhol couldn't even get in the garage.) She had on a white silk evening dress and a sleeveless mink jacket which, in a matter of weeks, was copied everyplace. She did the wildest dances in a dignified manner, no mean accomplishment when you consider that most of Killer Joe Piro's dances involved shaking oneself like a wet fox terrier. As the party wore on and the frenzy increased, here and there hip guests caught a sniff of pot, an odor which is yet to be detected in the White House. Later, there was something of a shouting match on the sidewalk in front of the Sign of the Dove between two men in their late twenties. It seems one had accused the other of stealing his boy friend, a crime not covered by the New York State Penal Code. Their shrill argument did not disturb the neighbors, who were used to that sort of thing, but the neighbors *did* complain most vigorously about the music that still issued from the Sign of the Dove at dawn.

While the names of almost everyone of interest who was Jackie's guest at the Sign of the Dove were wired around the world, no publication printed the name of (as it turned out) the most important guest, Aristotle Onassis. Actually, Mr. Onassis slipped in quietly in the middle of the party, caught Jackie's eye and waved, then turned around and walked right out. He did not take so much as a single glass of wine or a bite of food.

But the next day, when no reporter was around, Mr. Onassis visited Mrs. Kennedy's apartment and she told him all about the affair. This was the pattern of their almost clandestine friendship at the time. Ari insisted on staying well in the shadows, out of the columns. "For five years," Ari has told friends, "after President Kennedy died until Jackie and I got married, I was, insofar as public exposure with her went, the invisible man."

The gossip columnists seemed to overlook the fact that Ari was a regular caller in New York, that he several times accompanied Jackie to Hyannis Port, and that he took her out when she was staying at Joseph P. Kennedy's winter retreat in Palm Beach. It was only the movie fan magazines that reported Ari was seeing Jackie, and they even predicted that she would become his bride, which proves that, perhaps, movie magazines should be taken more seriously.

Several columnists said later that they thought maybe Ari was after Jackie, but they simply could not bring themselves to believe that this Mediterranean, this man of mystery, two inches shorter than Jackie, a divorced man and an international swinger could ever be accepted as a serious suitor by a woman who loomed as large in the American scheme of things as, well, the Statue of Liberty. The press was madly looking for a "proper" man to match with Jackie, and it reported her dates in detail:

That she arrived for lunch at La Côte Basque one day with Cecil Beaton, the set designer for *My Fair Lady,* and the more recent *Coco.* That she dined at the Colony one evening with former Deputy Defense Secretary Roswell Gilpatric, wearing a Bergdorf black broadtail coat-dress that buttoned down the middle and was lightweight in everything but price (a cool $5,000). That she attended the Ballets Africains with composer Gian-Carlo Menotti. That she went poking around the antique shops with author Truman Capote, who wrote *Breakfast at Tiffany's,* which Jackie adored, and also *In Cold Blood,* which she found hardly the thing for someone who had trouble getting to sleep. That she turned up for a party in Oliver Smith's elegant Brooklyn Heights town house (he's the stage designer) with Mike Nichols, the something-of-a-genius who directed *The Graduate.* That one night she had dinner with Kevin McCarthy, the actor, then went to a party in the Park Avenue apartment of Mr. and Mrs. Martin Gabel (Arlene Francis) that was knee-deep in U.S. Senators, movie producers, and just plain down-to-earth millionaires. As if that wasn't enough, columnists reported that Jackie and Kevin then went to Café Nicholson to attend another party, this one in honor of spooky cartoonist Charles Addams, and didn't buzz off until three in the morning.

The strange thing was that almost all of Jackie's escorts were of the sort who could be considered "safe." That is, none of them was regarded as a possible future hus-

band for the former First Lady. There were several
reasons for classifying them, by and large, "safe," and one
caustic socialite summed them up thus: "Jackie's dates are
all very married, or very old, or very queer."

Her regular escorts included married men, like the
above-mentioned Gilpatric, 61 at the time, who accompanied her on a trip to Yucatan; Arthur Schlesinger, Jr.,
52, the historian and loyal Kennedy follower; composer-
conductor Leonard Bernstein, 50, and former Defense
Secretary Robert McNamara, 52. Now, none of these
men, it is true, was really ancient, but, after all, Jackie
was in her thirties and, behind her dark glasses, could
pass for a young lady in her twenties, capable of distract-
ing a West Point parade into breaking ranks.

All of the married men listed here seemed immensely
honored to be escorting Mrs. Kennedy. But she really
didn't seem visibly to turn any of then on, *except* Mr.
McNamara, who now heads the World Bank. He was so
impressed that *Time* magazine wrote: "When Jackie's
around, *The Computer* [McNamara] turns into a puppy
dog wagging its tail."

Jackie had so many married escorts, who were apparently willing to leave the old lady at home watching
Bonanza, that the women's page of a Midwest newspaper
commented at the time: "When Jackie wants to go out,
she borrows other women's husbands as freely as the
woman next door borrows a cup of sugar."

Eyebrows were also raised because Jackie appeared at
the ballet, chic lunches, the theater, and at discreet private dinner parties with unmarried interior decorators,
dress designers, stage designers, and offbeat novelists who
were hardly the kind to settle down with a wife and a

built-in family, although they'd be perfectly at ease, as many were, during the summer months, on Fire Island with a bottle of Campari.

As the months went on, the press was dismayed that it could not link Jackie, with any reasonable degree of accuracy, with a dashing figure. ("CAROLINE AND JOHN-JOHN NEED A FATHER!" wailed the London *Daily Mirror*.) So the reporters made the most of what was available. An "affair" was whipped up between Jackie and Antonio Rodriguez y Diaz-Cañabate, 64, a widower and the Spanish Ambassador to the Vatican, when he showed Jackie around St. Peter's during her visit to Rome in the fall of 1967. When Jackie and the Ambassador were "linked" in the less reliable periodicals, her sister, Lee, said: "Oh, good Lord! The next thing you know they'll have Jackie in love with a survivor of the Battle of Bull Run."

Finally, the press agreed that, despite his fifty years, the man most likely to win Mrs. Kennedy was Britain's Lord Harlech, the former David Ormsby-Gore, who was the Ambassador to the United States when John Kennedy was in the White House. A handsome widower, Lord Harlech seemed to have a lot going for him. An aristocrat, he was as sophisticated and urbane as only a proper Britisher can be, and he had bits of money tucked away here and there. His ancestors had all been properly buried, and not one of them hanged, and all of them had earned the honors of the Imperial Realm.

The Jackie–Lord Harlech nonsense reached its height when Jackie, who hates traveling alone, was escorted by His Lordship to Cambodia, in 1967, where they inspected the ruins of Angkor Wat. The reporters, who stuck to them like flypaper during the trans-Pacific flight and the Asian odyssey, could detect nothing more romantic or intimate than the time Lord Harlech helped Jackie remove a pebble that had become wedged in her shoe during a walk across a gravel path.

"I was sent halfway around the world to cover a 'romance,'" said one disillusioned Chicago reporter, "and, hell, it's about as romantic as a tea party given by the Daughters of the American Revolution."

The press, and the curious nation, were truly schizophrenic about Jackie's private life. While on the one hand they were bursting to see their idol romantically involved, on the other hand they were shattered by the thought of John Kennedy's widow as the lifetime companion of another man. For them, there was no substitute for Camelot.

Everyone had an opinion on what Jackie should do. "The meddlesome millions," wrote Walter Winchell at the time, "could only be satisfied if the name of every man Jackie wants to date was first submitted to a national plebiscite." Another commentator, also sympathetic to Jackie, went one step further. He said that, judging by public opinion, anybody Mrs. Kennedy wanted to marry would no doubt have to be first approved by a Constitutional Amendment.

"I don't think anything can kill the magic of Jacqueline Kennedy," pontificated Dr. Joyce Brothers, a psychiatrist to the populace at large, "*unless*, perhaps, she remarries. As long as she remains John Kennedy's widow, she reminds us constantly of him. Jackie is the chief guardian of her husband's memory. If Jacqueline Kennedy *does* remarry, she will probably lose her place in the nation's heart."

If the good Dr. Brothers knew that at the moment she wrote her sermon-from-the-mount Jackie was contemplating marriage, and that the leading candidate was Aristotle Onassis, hardly a typical American boy, she would probably have had another go at her typewriter, crying, like the Red Queen in *Alice in Wonderland*, "Off with her head!"

Chapter Three

THE ROAD TO SKORPIOS

Perhaps Jackie and Ari didn't themselves know where they were going during the five years of their secret friendship as their lives and emotions became ever more deeply entwined. But Maria Callas, you can be sure, smelled something amiss.

One day, according to friends, she said to Mr. Onassis at a party in Ari's flat on Avenue Foch in Paris: "You *blanking, blanking* two-timing Greek *blank!* Being you can't buy, steal, or be elected to the Presidency of the United States, you want to marry a widow of a President to add to your collection!"

The moment of truth for Jackie and Ari apparently came in May, 1968, during another extended cruise aboard the *Christina*, with all its life of idle, carefree escapism. It was a long, easy cruise with only a few intimate friends.

Night after night, after dinner, as the host and Jackie nibbled white grapes, they listened, with a touch of melancholy, as the Greek musicians played and sang Ari's favorite ballad:

These are bitter summers,
And you have taught me to spend them with you.

At the end of that cruise Jackie, her mind made up, returned to America and told the Kennedy clan at a solemn gathering, not unlike an emergency joint meeting of the House and Senate, that she was going to marry Aristotle Onassis and would make the announcement public at a later date. They were stunned. As stunned as if Ted Kennedy had said that, the next time he ran for public office, he would run as a Republican.

The immediate reaction was: What will this do to the Kennedy image? No one for the moment thought about Jackie, and this she will *never* forget.

Lyndon Johnson had recently declared he would not again accept his party's nomination, and Senator Robert Kennedy, convinced that the Chicago convention would turn to him, said, when he had calmed down somewhat and regained his sense of humor: "For God's sake, Jackie, a thing like this could cost me five states!"

The pressure was immense. "The Kennedys," said one of Jackie's cousins, "did everything but kidnap Jackie and lock her up in a convent." As Cardinal Cushing, that old friend of the Kennedys, said later, there were appeals from within the family, and from other "high" sources, for him to intervene with Jackie, talk her out of this "ridiculous" affair. The Cardinal refused. He saw Jackie and told her it was her life to live, her happiness to consider, even though, by marrying a divorced man, she would be regarded, in the fine print of Roman Catholicism, as little better than a public sinner.

Eve Pollard, in her book *Jackie,* published in London, reported the situation thus: "When Jackie told her brother-in-law [Bobby] she was thinking of remarrying, he got hopping mad. In May of 1968 he was concentrating his efforts on a Presidential primary barnstorming the like of which had not been seen since his brother's efforts and success in 1960. And though willing to allow his sister-in-law everything, after all she had gone through, he could not take this. He entreated her to wait, at least until the Presidential election had come and gone. He hoped to avoid harm to the Kennedy image. He also hoped she would forget Onassis."

Finally, one day, in a scene that an Oscar-winning director would have been proud of, Ethel and Joan Kennedy came to Jackie's Fifth Avenue apartment, and they stood on that vast Oriental rug in that superb living room, and they pleaded their case with such a flow of tears that it seemed possible that the tenant underneath would complain of a leak.

Ethel and Joan begged Jackie to keep in mind their husbands' careers. They even got patriotic, and said: "Jackie, if you hurt our men by marrying *this* man, you will hurt the America they have been raised to serve!"

Once again, the only person not being given a thought was Jackie Kennedy. Where did she fit in the Kennedy pattern? What they were telling her, in so many words, was that the widow of John Fitzgerald Kennedy could never, never again sleep with another man.

To put it bluntly, Jackie Kennedy practically shoved Ethel and Joan Kennedy out of her apartment. And, a few days later, reviewing the trying visit with friends, she said: "The way Ethel and Joan acted, you'd think I was going to marry Frankenstein, instead of one of the sweetest men in the world."

However, Jackie and Ari decided to compromise, and continued to guard their secret, to go along with the Kennedys, for the moment at least. Then Bobby was slain, and two weeks before Election Day, Mrs. Hugh Auchincloss, Jackie's mother, issued a formal statement to the effect that her daughter would marry Mr. Aristotle Socrates Onassis, of Athens, Greece, and Buenos Aires, Argentina, and that was the ball game.

When the news flashed around the world, the reaction could only be described by saying: All hell broke loose. JACKIE HOW COULD YOU? headlined Stockholm's *Expressen.* Cracked Bob Hope: "Nixon has a Greek running mate, now everyone wants one."

Paris' *Le Monde* editorialized: "Jackie, whose staunch courage during John's funeral made such an impression, now chooses to shock by marrying a man who could be her father and whose career contradicts, rather strongly, to say the least, the liberal spirit that animated President Kennedy."

"German women saw a halo around her head," said Hamburg's illustrated weekly, *Stern,* "but now it is gone with the wind."

The breast beating was a case history of what happens when a celebrity falls—or seems to fall—off her pedestal. The twenty-three-year age difference between Ari and Jackie was made much of. It was recalled that when Stavros Niarchos married automotive heiress Charlotte Ford, also twenty-three years *his* junior, Mr. Onassis, lacking foresight, had commented: "Poor fellow, he's going through a change of life."

The usually talkative Kennedys suffered a severe attack of silence. Rose Kennedy wasn't taking calls from anybody. Twenty-four hours later Senator Edward Kennedy issued a statement congratulating Jackie and Ari that was as rigidly formal and devoid of personal warmth as a Presidential endorsement of a candidate for county sheriff.

There was a goodly percentage of the more thoughtful population who thought it a disgrace that few people in public life, besides Cardinal Cushing, were willing to come out and say that, no matter how you sliced it, it *was* Jackie's life.

It took Lee Radziwill, however, to dispose of most of the self-righteous opposition by saying, a couple of weeks later, "If Jackie's new husband had been blond, rich, young, and *Anglo-Saxon*, most Americans would have been much happier."

A couple of nights after the wedding announcement, ninety passengers were bounced off Onassis-owned Olympic Airways Flight 412 to Athens. They were told to disembark, just like that. The plane was then occupied by Jackie; her children, John and Caroline; her sister, Lee; her mother; and two Kennedys, Mrs. Peter Lawford and Mrs. Stephen Smith. Reporters with binoculars, watching the embarkation from behind police lines, searched vainly for Ted Kennedy, for Rose, for Ethel or Joan.

For forty-eight hours, the wedding site, Ari's private island of Skorpios in its indigo sea, was the news center of the world, although the closest most journalists got was a view from the deck of a chartered boat or aircraft.

Outside the door of the tiny Chapel of the Holy Virgin, as is customary in wedding services of the Greek Orthodox Church, Aristotle Onassis waited for his bride to arrive.

When she drove up, accompanied by her mother, her sisters-in-law, and her children, he kissed her on both cheeks, and they walked together down the aisle to the altar, which held a Bible and two rings. Each held a burning candle. The air in the chapel was heavy with incense, and the Byzantine gold ikons glittered in the candlelight.

Ari wore a businessman's double-breasted dark blue suit, a white shirt, and a red tie. In his buttonhole was a lemon blossom. Jackie's white gown was very short, and pleated; her hair, tied back with a white ribbon, was full and high.

Ari held Jackie's right hand in his right hand. Caroline and John, Jr. and their new stepbrother and stepsister Alexander and Christina Onassis, stood in the aisle behind them.

Hymns were sung in Greek and prayers were said, by a heavily bearded priest, in Greek and English. Then the rings—one for Ari, one for Jackie—were exchanged three times, hand to hand, by the priest, who said: "The Servant of God, Aristotle, is wedlocked with the Servant of God, Jacqueline, in the name of the Father, the Son, and the Holy Ghost."

Two white leather "wedding crowns"—with twigs and buds—were passed slowly over the couple's heads. Then Jackie and Ari took three sips of red wine and, holding hands with the priest, danced around the altar three times.

(At this point one guest, who had had *more* than three sips of wine, whispered, in a very British accent: "It's all so bloody barbaric.")

That was that, and the guests, led by young John and Caroline, rushed forward and pelted the couple with rice and sugared almonds—rice for fertility, sugar for happiness.

The following week, when the United States calmed down and got off its high horse, when, in the light of reason, people realized that, really, the Madonna hadn't run off with Jack the Ripper, logic began to prevail. *Vogue* had this to say: "The announcement of her marriage to Mr. Onassis, an international figure of power—granitic, laughing, adamant—came as a fist blow to her public all over the world who had been supremely happy on the lovely myths they had devised for themselves. The actual woman is far better—delectable, determined, emotional, strongly beautiful, questing. She can again be herself, eager to exult, prepared for exaltation, living in her natural element of vital excitement."

Columnist Suzy said: "They were made for each other. She can give him what he needs; he can give her what she needs. What greater celebrity in the world to collect than Jackie Kennedy? She's a living legend."

Paul O'Neil, writing in *Life,* sounded a hopeful note when he said: "There was something about the union which deserved to be weighed. All marriages involve some kind of balance of emotional power—or the lack of it. What other man could marry Jackie Kennedy without simultaneously being dominated by her and the memory of her departed husband? What other man, in fact, could dump her, if he chose to later, without being destroyed by public opinion?

"But what other woman—so splendid a woman of accomplishment and self-esteem—could be so utterly indispensable even to a bauble-collecting billionaire? How could they fail, in short—though they fought like wildcats for the next decade—to live happily ever after?"

The wedding, in the usual Onassis manner, was not done on the cheap. Most of the forty guests had crossed the Atlantic at Ari's expense, and for each one he had a valuable gift. Jackie's mother, Mrs. Hugh Auchincloss, received a charming diamond clip. There were also liberal gifts to the minister, the church, and cash handouts to the police guards and to the many old retainers on Skorpios. Ari is the "Duke of Skorpios," and, once again, he was acting in the manner of the dukes of antiquity who believed in sharing their pleasure with their serfs.

Two hairdressers had been flown to Skorpios to keep the ladies' tresses properly in place, and a special butcher to cut the meat just so, a masseuse, two extra chefs, a *bouzouki* orchestra, and a pair of Greece's best singers of native songs. Reporters who studied the matter placed the total cost, excluding gifts, around $40,500.

Chapter Four

JACKIE MARRIED THE JET SET

When Jacqueline Kennedy married Aristotle Onassis she was not only taking on a new husband, she was taking on a new way of life, the life of the international jet set. Unless we understand jet-set thinking on marriage and morals and money, we can never understand the Ari-Jackie marriage. People in the jet set, discussing Ari and Jackie, don't mention the word "love." Love is for kids; Ari was sixty-two; Jackie, thirty-nine. And love is for squares.

The idea of a thing called "love" impelling two otherwise apparently sane human beings to give up everything else, as millions do, and settle down, perhaps in North Platte, Nebraska, and immediately start producing children, and spending the evening before the television set, and buying things on time—well, in the jet set a life like that is regarded as—well, it just isn't regarded.

Certainly, jet setters don't marry for love. And certainly not for sex. The jet set is the Beautiful People, who don't believe they were made beautiful to be admired behind glass. In the jet set you don't have to marry for sex; sex is everyplace, as available as a dry Martini, on the rocks or straight up.

The thinking *is* different. A man like Aristotle Onassis, who has been around forever, it seems, with the most captivating females in existence, is no sinner, by his standards. Mr. Onassis is not immoral—he is *amoral*. Amoral in the courtly, old-European sense, when it was considered quite proper for a gentleman to have a mistress tucked away in a little *pied-à-terre*. The fact that the gentleman had a mistress, and was quite fond of her, in no way detracted from his loyalty to his wife. More often than not, the wife was quite aware of her husband's extramarital involvement, and paid it no serious heed; some things are best ignored.

The same unwritten code of conduct is the norm in international society today, and it is applicable to both sexes. If a jet-set husband came home unexpectedly one night and found his wife knotted around another man he would say, in the manner of his kind: "Oh, I'm sorry to have disturbed you. I'll be in touch later." Such an encounter would not result in any middle-class, Levit-townish wailing and abuse. There would be no self-pity and cries of: "How you've hurt me!" No flying of fists and articles of furniture. None of the emotionalism that would be par for the course among the less sophisticated and less broad-minded citizenry.

Those who really know Jackie and Ari think that sex has not been a major factor in their relationship. If we eliminate love and sex as reasons for Jackie's marriage to

Ari, than what have they found in each other? What can they give each other?

First, let us remember that opposites attract—and Ari and Jackie are opposites. Jackie represents the security of old families, of stability, of a life dictated by certain laws and conventions. Ari represents the world of the dispossessed, of upheaval, the life of the freebooter whose only law is the law of survival. (One time Mr. Onassis said: "To make your way, you must sometimes be prepared to see your nearest and dearest go to hell.")

Jackie had always missed the kind of freedom from social and family obligations that one finds in the jet set. One time she said, wistfully: "Oh, to have been born a *nothing*, and to have nothing to live up to." On the other hand, Ari has shown an increasing desire, in recent years, to begin a family dynasty—and he resents the fact that his own background is so undistinguished. Once, in a philosophical mood, he said: "If one had several generations of established family behind one, if one *really* had roots, it would give life more of a purpose."

But, in reality, the main thing Jackie and Ari could give —and *have* given—each other is companionship. Not a passive companionship—and this is important—but a *high-spirited* companionship, with a partner who never grumps or sulks, who sees humor in every situation, who realizes, every minute of the day, that every human being on earth is heading directly for the grave, and that the thing to do while one is alive is *live*.

This attitude was expressed with fine clarity one night by Winston Churchill, who was one of Onassis' good friends. It was during the most trying days of World War II. The Germans were blitzing England by air. London was burning. Mr. Churchill and several of his colleagues watched the destruction of their beloved central city from the roof of Number 10 Downing Street. The city—perhaps the war—seemed lost. Then, suddenly, the Prime Minister looked at his watch and said: "It's getting on. Let us go downstairs. War or no war, one must never miss one's dinner." (Mr. Onassis, like Sir Winston, has a kind of gallows sense of humor. One ancient joke that he often tells goes like this: "What's the noisiest thing in the world? Two skeletons making love on a tin roof.")

Aristotle Onassis, except when he's talking money, is never heavy, never a drag. What a relief for Jackie, after the earnest intellectuals and politicians who surrounded and perpetually bored and irritated her during the Kennedy years!

A while back, the black novelist and polemicist James Baldwin said: "I've been to too many funerals. I can't laugh anymore." God knows, Jackie has been to her share of funerals. But her new husband has convinced her that life goes on. Now she's laughing more than ever before.

Jackie Onassis, her friends say, has stopped being a realist in the American-Calvinistic face-the-truth sense of the word. Mr. Onassis has sold her on *his* idea of a realist: "A realist," says Ari, "is a man who believes in miracles."

Jackie has seldom looked at a newspaper since Bobby was killed. And she won't hear a word about politics. "I will tell you everything I know," Aristotle Onassis told her on that day, in 1968, when she agreed to marry him. "Except for one thing—I will never tell you bad news."

A full week passed before Ari told his wife about Teddy Kennedy's accident at Chappaquiddick Island, in which a young secretary who had been a campaign worker for Bobby was killed. When Ari finally told her, he did so only because, as he explained to a reporter, "we expected

Senator Kennedy to come here and take his vacation with us. Now he probably won't be able to make it. Poor man, he has had his share of bad luck."

What woman would not be delighted to have a husband who never brings home anything except smiles? "Trouble," Mr. Onassis often says, "should stop at a man's front door."

One day in the summer of 1969 Mr. Onassis received a financial kick in the teeth when a $400,000,000 deal he had been negotiating with the ruling military junta in Greece collapsed (at least temporarily). Mr. and Mrs. Onassis had house guests that night, and Jackie and the guests were already having their cocktails when Ari, a mite late, flew home to Skorpios from his office in Athens, landing on the front lawn in his private helicopter. One of the guests present that night told me, some time later: "Ari seemed in wonderful humor. He danced with all the ladies— did a kookie Greek folk dance with Jackie—and he acted as if everything in his life was coming up roses. None of us knew of Ari's setback with the junta until we read about it in the newspapers the next day."

How refreshing is a man like that to Jackie, who has always been an ardent escapist. Her life with Ari is concocted of such pure, fairy-tale glamour that she must remember life in the White House, and her husband's eternal concern with social problems, as a big fat bore. One time one of Jackie's oldest friends said: "Jackie has the social consciousness of Louis XIV."

John Kennedy did not have Ari's ability to leave his troubles in the office. The talkative members of the White House domestic staff often whispered, in the corridors and employees' mess, that when Mr. and Mrs. Kennedy dined alone, the President would often complain and groan about his tremendous responsibilities and problems, from the first bite of food to the last sip of coffee. This really nettled Jackie, who never felt that she was married to the faceless electorate. In fact, she was more than somewhat jealous of the people of the United States. She simply could not regard national problems as *her* problems. One night, according to a gossipy White House butler, just when a succulent roast had been served, the President suddenly exclaimed, dead serious: "What in hell am I ever going to do about air pollution?"

Disgusted, Jackie said: "It's very simple, my dear. Get the Air Force to spray our industrial centers with Chanel Number Five."

Despite the jet-set gaiety surrounding Jackie, there are still physical reminders of the violence that took her first husband from her. Whenever Jackie leaves the house there is always a bodyguard nearby. Secret Service protection for the former First Lady ended in March of 1968, though Caroline and John will be guarded until they are sixteen. While Jackie is in New York, Mr. Onassis has to pay the Pinkerton Detective Agency, and other private-eye outfits, at the rate of $7.50 an hour for round-the-clock protection, or $1,260 a week.

One reason for the bodyguards is that ever since her marriage to Mr. Onassis Jackie has been the target of a certain amount of hate mail. And a few times she has been personally abused. One day in Paris, two springs ago, Jackie, waiting for her husband, who was attending a business conference in the George V Hotel, was taking an *apéritif* by herself at a sidewalk table in front of Fouquet's on the Champs Elysées. An American couple, who had apparently drunk a heavy lunch, stopped and stared at her. Finally the woman, who was constructed along the lines of a stuffed laundry bag, asked:

"Aren't you Jackie Onassis?"

"Yes."

"You should be ashamed of yourself, marrying a foreigner!"

Later that evening Ari and Jackie dined with old Newport friends and Jackie told of the earlier incident. She concluded by saying that, for the first time in her life, she was sorry she had not studied karate.

Jackie has somehow managed to live with vicious letter writers, and with bodyguards. One time when she was at New York's Colony restaurant, Jackie discussed the guards who were always nearby. "I guess the theme song of my life," said Jackie, "is that oldie, *Me and My Shadow.*"

Mr. Onassis takes no chances. Besides the bodyguards always a few steps behind Jackie, armed men guard the villas at Glyfada and Skorpios with, it is said, everything but land mines and booby traps. Security of all kinds comes to $84,000 a year.

It sometimes seems, these days, that Mr. Onassis is the producer of a play—and Jackie is the only member of the audience. When Ari invites people to one of their homes, or to the *Christina,* he does so with only one thought in mind—they *must* amuse Jackie. He often invites people like Rudi Nureyev, the ballet dancer, and after dinner Rudi puts on a one-man show for Jackie, whom he adores. Or the British comedienne Beatrice Lillie, who will sing something like:

> *I hate everything pretty,*
> *I despise Radio City.*

The parade of guests is really something. Best-selling authors, ex-kings, movie stars, Olympic athletes, international vagrants—the Beautiful People. With such people at her table, Jackie must shudder when she recalls some of those stuffy dinners in the White House. Like the night she had to make small talk with the Ambassador of a new African country who kept saying, in a monotone, as if announcing the departure of a train: "In my country we have rhinoceroses."

How could dinner with the nine old men of the Supreme Court compare with dinner with the bubbling, batty cast of *Hair*, even with all their clothes on? Ari, of course, would know how to handle the Supreme Court—*and* the cast of *Hair*. He never lets down for a minute; he is one of the most charming men on earth. Mrs. Frank McMahon, wife of the Canadian multi-millionaire industrialist, said: "Ari can charm the birds out of the trees and make them sing *Tea for Two* in Greek." "Ari is more fun than a roomful of monkeys," said the Duke of Windsor, one time, absolutely fracturing himself at his own joke.

The best story to illustrate Jackie today concerns a visit she made to the island of Corfu, during the summer of 1969, with Mrs. Basil Goulandris, whose husband also is a multimillionaire Greek shipping operator. The two women sat outside a local *taverna* and Jackie, who was wearing jeans and a floppy pullover, kicked off her shoes. At that moment a photographer approached and Jackie gave him permission to snap her. Laughing, Jackie turned to Mrs. Goulandris and said: "Imagine if I had been photographed in bare feet when we were in the White House! The President—I can just hear him now—would have roared: 'For God's sake, Jackie, are you trying to make sure I don't get re-elected?'"

An excellent comment on "the marriage of the century," as some headline writers put it, was made by author Gore Vidal, who is related to Jackie on the Auchincloss side, and who was practically raised side-by-side with her at Newport. Mr. Vidal, also an old friend of Aristotle Onassis, said: "Onassis is dynamic and protective, and I think that is what Jackie needs. Not so much physical protection, but a certain kind of warm, fatherly affection. Though she's independent, she's very brittle. She needs someone who will give her a thicker lining. I think Onassis is doing this for her. Jackie is *very happy* with Onassis —perhaps more than with her first husband. . . . John Kennedy was wrapped up in himself and his career. She was like another room at the White House—almost a prisoner. Can an omnivorous, rich businessman of sixty-four find happiness with an attractive woman of forty? The answer is YES!"

Although Jackie has embraced the jet set with enthusiasm, it must be made clear that she does not necessarily embrace jet set morals. There has never been one breath of scandal about Jackie, not when she was Miss Bouvier, not when she was Mrs. John F. Kennedy, and not since she has been Mrs. Aristotle Onassis. One must remember that during her entire life, most of which has been closely scrutinized by the press, there has never been one known indiscretion. Jacqueline Onassis, it appears, is simply one of those women who has never played the game of musical beds, a game that is standard operating procedure in the social worlds she has been so much a part of.

People who knew Jackie in finishing school, then as a debutante in Newport and New York, then as a newspaper gal in Washington remember her, in a phrase popular twenty years ago, as a "hold your meter, driver" type. In other words, after a young man took her to a theater or a movie or a night club, and then took her home in a hack, she would always say, as the vehicle pulled up in front of her address: "Hold your meter, driver." Her escort was being told, in no uncertain terms, "Good night," and any hope he might have had of being invited in was shot down, then and there.

A man now affluent and prominent in the security market is quite willing to discuss the many times he was Jackie's companion during her sub-deb and deb years, right up to the time she met the then Senator Kennedy. "Jackie was always great fun," he says. "But as for making a pass—forget it! One would no more make a pass at Jacqueline Bouvier than one would make a pass at the statue of Marie Antoinette in Mme. Tussaud's Wax Museum."

Of course, those were more sedate times; but even then people listed in the Social Register kind of expected a young lady to have an occasional fling. The tolerant attitude of high society on such matters was recorded by Stephen Birmingham in his delightful book on upper-crust foibles, *The Right People*. A society matron told Mr. Birmingham: "I told my daughter that if she wants to have a fling with a stranger, for goodness sake, have it. But not for a minute is she to entertain the thought of marrying him."

To change focus for a moment, remember that young John Kennedy himself, a virile and attractive man, never pretended to be an Eagle Scout when it came to the opposite sex. In fact, the late, lamented *Saturday Evening Post* once surveyed his private life in an article titled "The Senate's Gay Bachelor."

"It is not true," Bobby Kennedy once told some friends, "that Jack made out with all the girls in the District of Columbia. There wasn't enough time!"

Another time of her life when Jackie surprised her friends by her near-Victorian habits was during the year she spent as a student at the Sorbonne in Paris. Scott Fitzgerald himself said, some years ago, that "when an American girl goes to the Sorbonne she is bound to learn at least two things—French and *wow!*" When Jackie arrived at the Sorbonne, prim and pretty, to every French boy she was a classic example of the most cherished dream, a rich American heiress, and they moved in with Gallic aggressiveness. During strolls through the Luxembourg Gardens and picnic trips to the glorious countryside around Versailles, the young Frenchmen insisted that Jackie give them her favors, as if it were their national right. Each time Jackie proved she had the evasive tactics of a broken-field runner.

When John Kennedy was nominated for the Presidency in 1960, a reporter for a Paris paper looked up some of Jackie's former schoolmates at the Sorbonne. From one of her contemporaries he elicited this recollection: "When it came to *l'amour*, Jackie was like the Mona Lisa. The smile was inviting, but *don't touch!*"

All of her life Jackie had money—but never enough. Her father, John Vernon Bouvier, was short of cash after the stock market took a dive in 1929. Her stepfather, Hugh Auchincloss, had plenty of money, but basically he was very conservative, and he was damned if he was going to let his two expensive stepdaughters, Jackie and Lee, go flinging it around, something they were and are quite expert at doing.

(When Jackie had a job in Washington, just before marrying John Kennedy, she earned $52 a week. Her weekly expenditure for clothes alone was $75.)

John Kennedy tried, as best he could, to keep Jackie from buying all the dresses and all the jewels in Paris, London, Rome, and New York. He did everything but lock the First Lady in her room to keep her from making headlines with her compulsive shopping sprees. (The President once asked a friend: "Isn't there a Shoppers Anonymous?")

When John Kennedy died, his will was in order, and he took good care of Jackie. (She never really got any money from her own family. Her father died pretty nearly broke, and her mother, who is quite wealthy, is somewhat remote. Jackie and her mother, as one of their mutual acquaintances says, "are forever walking on each other's nerves.")

A large portion of the money John Kennedy left his family—a trust fund that brings in around $250,000 a year—is earmarked for the use of the children, and Jackie must give the trustees full financial accountings. There have been some horrendous hassles in the Kennedy family office on Park Avenue between Jackie, who can't remember what she paid for *anything*, and "the keepers of the loot," as she calls the trustees, among other things.

Not long ago I learned that one of the Kennedy family's head bookkeepers could not understand an item for $2,000 listed for the month of September, 1969, under "allowance." When he queried Mrs. Onassis about this, she hesitated a moment, then replied: "That must be for John's allowance."

The bookkeeper, trying to retain his composure, asked:

"You mean, Mrs. Onassis, that an eight-year-old spent $2,000 in September?"

Jackie admitted: "It does seem a bit high for John, at that."

Jackie, I was told, has not yet been able to figure out exactly what happened to the missing $2,000.

Unlike the Kennedys, with their determination to itemize every cent spent, Mr. Onassis no more expects Jackie to keep books than he expects her to take a job in a tractor factory to help pay the grocery bill. "Jackie can have anything she wants, if it makes her happy," he says, copying, to some extent, the late Damon Runyon, who once declared: "Money has a tendency to buy happiness." And, it takes an awful lot of money to make Jackie happy—millions and millions.

PART TWO

The

$20,000,000

Honeymoon

Chapter Five

SPEND! SPEND! SPEND!

When Jackie married Ari a British newspaper ran this headline: JACKIE MARRIES A BLANK CHECK. How true! Right now Mr. and Mrs. Aristotle Socrates Onassis are spending more money than any other couple on this earth. Their personal expenditures are running at the rate of $20,000,000 annually.

That's more, by far, than it costs the British government to maintain Queen Elizabeth and her consort, Prince Philip. The Queen gets an annual allowance from the state of $1,140,000, and the Prince is paid $96,000—a total of only $1,236,000. Mr. Onassis hasn't been talking poor mouth lately, but the royal couple is really crying. Prince Philip says that he and his wife are running into the red, and, to make ends meet, the Prince has already sold a small yacht, "and I shall probably have to give up polo, pretty soon, and things like that." Furthermore, unless the royal couple can put their hands on maybe another $500,000 a year they'll have to move out of Buckingham Palace, according to the Prince, and find a smaller place to live. (One of their problems is that Buckingham Palace and Windsor Castle and other "homes of the realm" cost a fortune to keep from falling apart because they're so ancient and decrepit and run-down and drafty *and* the roofs leak—why, Queen Elizabeth's insecticide bill alone must be a whopper!)

But when you come down to it, is anybody surprised that Jackie is now spending more money than the Queen of England? What did any of us expect? One fast-moving member of the jet set, the gracious Lady Sarah Spencer-Churchill, whose brother, the Marquess of Blandford (the next Duke of Marlborough), is married to Tina Livanos Onassis, Ari's first wife—yes, things get a bit complicated in the jet set—told me: "Mr. and Mrs. Onassis are certainly spending more money this year than anyone in international society by far. I know. I've seen them in Paris, London, New York, Nassau, and Athens, during the course of the year, and, believe me, the sky is the limit." (Lady Sarah, by the way, is currently married to a young Greek actor, the talented Theo Roubanis.)

Nobody will argue with Lady Sarah—Ari is spending incredible sums to maintain himself and his spouse in a style that would have aroused the envy of the Czars of Russia. And Jackie, who was never known to pinch her pennies, is buying every available goodie at such a rate that, when we stack up how she lives alongside the way that Cleopatra, who was no slouch, used to live, we can only conclude that by comparison Cleopatra was a welfare case.

Now, anyone who can do long division will figure out that to spend $20,000,000 a year one must spend $384,-615.38 a week. Offhand, this sounds like a pleasant but practically impossible undertaking, unless one goes for broke at Las Vegas, or goes around giving away $1,000,-000 handouts to passing strangers.

But even at that rate of spending, there is no need to worry about the Onassises. They are *not* dipping into capital.

Financial publications have estimated Onassis' annual income from shipping *alone* to be $50,000,000 a year, and he has pieces of the action in several other industries, plus a portfolio of stocks so large that if they were dumped on the market the Dow Jones averages would go into a tailspin.

Several years ago Onassis refused a reporter's request for an interview by saying: "I simply do not have the time. My time is worth $200,000 a day."

Accepting Ari's own statement of how much he makes daily, that would give him a weekly income of $1,000,000 for a five-day, forty-hour week, not counting overtime, and the man puts in at least sixty hours each week. So actually the Onassises are living well within their income, which is an unusual and admirable accomplishment these days, and they're putting aside a few dollars for their old age.

Actually, Ari could retire right now and he and Jackie would not have to cut their cost of living one cent. Many financial observers, here and abroad, have stated that if Mr. Onassis liquidated all his holdings he would be worth from $500,000,000 to one billion. Take the lower figure, $500,000,000. If that sum were put into the friendly neighborhood bank, it would bring, at the usual five percent interest, an annual return of $25,000,000 a year.

So much for the income. How about the outgo? Well, when you come down to it, $20,000,000 a year can be spent without straining, if you have enough homes scattered around the globe and enough servants to maintain them properly. Let's check out Onassis' places of residence, which are kept ever-ready for occupancy and fully staffed.

There is a villa in Monte Carlo, with seven servants standing by. A Paris penthouse, five servants. A hacienda in Montevideo, Uruguay, thirty-eight servants. A villa at Glyfada, in the suburbs of Athens, ten servants. Jackie's Fifth Avenue apartment in New York, five servants. The private island of Skorpios in the Ionian Sea, seventy-two servants; islands are not as easy to keep spick-and-span as efficiency apartments. The yacht *Christina*, which has a sixty-five-man crew, plus a seaplane pilot and a doctor always on duty. If that isn't enough, there are permanent hotel suites in New York's Pierre and in London's Claridge's. As you can see, it is doubtful that Ari and Jackie will ever find themselves without a roof over their heads and thus have to split and spend the night at the YWCA and YMCA.

Every one of Mr. Onassis' domiciles is stocked with a complete set of his clothes and a toothbrush and safety razor. This makes it possible for him, when the impulse grabs him, to take a taxi to the nearest airport and fly to any of his homes without having to pack a bag. Soon these domiciles will also be stocked with a complete Jackie wardrobe which, at the rate she collects wearables, will mean that each home will have to be expanded, at least in the matter of closets. In fact, it was learned from a contractor in Athens that a special closet—perhaps it should be called a warehouse—is being constructed on Skorpios to hold the new things Jackie has bought since the wedding.

Now, as to servants. All told, Ari has 202 on his payroll, and most of them have remained passively in his service for many years. This should interest anybody who has encountered difficulty finding *one* reliable domestic without a communicable disease or distressing outward signs of total insanity.

The Onassis entourage includes a tailor, to operate the *Christina's* dry-cleaning plant, and three French chefs. Their salaries run from $250 a week, for the Manhattan-based chef, down to $100 a month for the slaveys in Greece. Being very conservative, if we say that $300 a month is the average paycheck, and multiply that by 202, we get $60,600 a month, or $727,200 annually, in salaries, which sounds like the budget of a Hilton hotel. Also, it should be remembered, most of Ari's domestic hands live in, and their food and lodging and unemployment insurance average $125 a head each month—a $25,250 monthly total, a $303,000 annual total.

Besides salaries and living expenses for this army of retainers, there are many unbudgeted, unpredictable costs. Mr. Onassis, being an employer in the feudal, lord-of-the-manor cut, has long made it a custom to assume the entire expenses for any domestic who becomes pregnant while under his roof. Because of this generosity, Ari is financing a small population explosion on his own, and the back quarters of his larger homes often resemble maternity wards. Being tolerant on such matters, Mr. Onassis does not insist that the servant in a family way be married; he only insists that the servant be female.

Ari's paternalism truly runs from the cradle to the grave; he pensions off those too old or too feeble to work, and when one dies he pays for the funeral and sends flowers to the bereaved widow. And there is another impossible-to-audit cost involved with the retention of so many menials. Mr. Onassis never remains very long at any one of his places, and, under the unwritten rules of absentee landlordship, the domestics are inclined to regard the boss's property as something less than sacred. Heaven knows how many crates of whiskey and haunches of beef are annually purloined from his wine cellars and freezers.

One time, a few years ago, Mr. Onassis asked one of his gardeners on Skorpios why, despite the large number of outdoor beds and hothouses, so few flowers were produced that when a party was given on the *Christina*, moored at Skorpios, it was necessary to import flowers from the mainland. The gardener complained about poor soil and poor weather. Mr. Onassis was not satisfied with this alibi, and he asked one of his private detectives (a billionaire needs them) to look into the matter. A few weeks later the mystery was solved. The gardener had been secretly exporting to one of Athens' most prestigious flower shops a veritable botanical garden of flowers. The shop was owned by his uncle.

I figure that the cost of Ari's servants' medical care, pregnancies, Social Security, pension funds, funerals, etc. —plus what they probably steal—comes to $150 a head a month, or $363,600 a year. Total annual bill for servants: $1,393,800.

While none of the Onassises' wealthy friends, to the best of anyone's knowledge, can match them in the number of domestics, their pals, by and large, do not exactly

have to do their own laundry. In the Aga Khan's houses
in Paris, Deauville, London, Sardinia, and in the south of
France (most of which Ari has visited), there are a total
of a hundred servants to do the little things necessary to
make life tolerable for him and his new bride, Lady Sarah
Crichton-Stuart.

Another Onassis friend, Mrs. Merriweather Post, the
cereal heiress, has in Palm Beach a 115-room cottage,
Mar-a-lago. Therein labor, among others, three chefs—
one for meat, one for pastry, one for candy. And there are
four secretaries; Mrs. Post maintains a furious correspon-
dence—letters to friends *and* a heavy volume of letters to
the editor, bitching about taxes. (Mr. Onassis has expressed his admiration for Mrs. Post's organizational
abilities.) Mar-a-lago is staffed in three eight-hour shifts.
Writer Ruth West, a recent visitor, said: "If a guest
hankers for homemade ice cream at 3 A.M., a ring will
bring it. A ring will also bring a masseur or, at any time,
your own chauffeured car. Mrs. Post's living expenses are
estimated to be $2,000,000 a year."

Not bad—but *not* Onassis.

Now contemplate the upkeep of the Onassises' far-
flung homes, *exclusive* of servants. Monthly maintenance
on Jackie's $200,000 co-operative Fifth Avenue apart-
ment is $750, according to real estate brokers, and
that's a minor matter. The New York hotel bill is $2,500
a month; in London, it's $1,200. Houses must be painted,
broken windows replaced, fixtures repaired, light bulbs
changed, driveways repaved, the refrigerators and wine
cellars regularly replenished, and trees injured in storms
nursed back to health. In fact, Mr. Onassis pays more
money to tree surgeons each year than ninety percent of
the American people pay for personal medical services.

All told, my accountant tells me, to maintain these eight land-based addresses in tip-top shape—Skorpios alone has six hundred acres—$2,000,000 a year would not be excessive.

A subject that does not amuse Mr. Onassis is taxes; in fact, like Mrs. Post, he would like to write petulant letters to the editor about them. Mr. Onassis is an expert at avoiding income taxes. But he is helpless when it comes to avoiding the land, highway, water, and school taxes that hound every homeowner. This, adjusted to the overall value of his various establishments, must be at least another round $2,000,000 a year.

Years ago, the story goes, the financier J. P. Morgan, snorting through his prominent nose, said: "Anyone who asks how much it costs to run a yacht can't afford one."

Well, Mr. Onassis wouldn't tell me how much it cost *him* to run his yacht; for one thing, he probably doesn't know. So I took the problem of the *Christina*'s upkeep to the New York editors of *Yachting* magazine, the bible of that luxury recreation, and I was told that their rule of thumb is this: It costs annually fifteen to twenty-five percent of the current value of a yacht for maintenance. The *Christina*, a onetime Canadian navy frigate, is estimated to be worth, considering the many improvements, a good $5,-700,000. At twenty percent, that brings its annual upkeep to something like $1,140,000.

Now, about art. Experts agree that Jackie and Ari own between them $25,000,000 in various forms of art. And, in the last year, they've acquired another $887,000 worth. Their Paris penthouse is chock-full of Louis XV and Louis XVI furniture, some pieces of which are signed by Nadal, furniture-maker for Marie Antoinette, who was

probably the original jet setter. Ari owns a bejeweled
Buddha worth, if a price can be placed on such things,
over $200,000. (It's the oldest statue of its kind in the
Western world.) Mr. Onassis is also the owner of a
gallery of paintings of the great masters, including an
El Greco acquired for $250,000. And in the villa at Gly-
fada there are many priceless Greek statues straight out
of antiquity. Many depict athletes of the Spartan school;
some wrestle with boys, some with girls.

Onassis, with all the publicity about his millions, is
naturally a target for every burglar, second-story man, pick-
pocket, and jewel thief known to authorities from Scotland
Yard to Tokyo's Central Investigation Bureau. Through
the years almost every one of Mr. Onassis' homes has
been robbed, and not always by professionals. Three years
ago a messenger boy was collared by one of Ari's private
detectives as he walked out of the Paris flat with a $4,000
Fabergé cigarette box in the pocket of his leather jacket.
And last year a temporary maid was seized as she left the
New York apartment wearing one of Jackie's mink coats
under her own cloth coat. In neither case were charges
pressed; more publicity, it was felt, would merely have
given more people larcenous aspirations.

Not too long ago a reporter asked an inspector of detectives in Athens if his outfit was keeping a protective
eye on the Onassises and their possessions. "Of a cer-
tainty," said the inspector. "It seems that every half-
demented creep, when he gets up in the morning, starts
thinking of new ways to relieve Mr. and Mrs. Onassis of
some of their things. We have, in the last year, arrested
several rather harmless crackpots and get-rich-quick
schemers, and together with Interpol we are investigating

a European kidnaping ring that, we understand, has been compiling information on the Onassises' residences and movements."

(Several veteran journalists in Athens know something of these ominous incidents, but Greece today is under a collective dictatorship, and the press is tightly censored; any subject that would displease Mr. Onassis, a favorite of the regime, is unlikely to get into print.)

Among the jet setters who frequent Athens these days, the idea that someone would think of snatching Jackie is no surprise. "After all," said one Greek-American socialite, rather proudly, "who else but Aristotle Onassis could pay a billion dollars in ransom and still be solvent?" Elmer Letterman, one of America's best-known insurance men, said: "People like Onassis are 'high risk'—and must pay accordingly." Another expert in the field told me that, to insure his possessions, as well as his life and his wife's life and the lives of their children, against fire, theft, flood, kidnaping, murder, and the measles, Mr. Onassis is shelling out at least $1,906,000 a year in premiums.

While insurance companies, for a price, will protect centimillionaires against anything from being mugged in the bathtub to being bitten by a zebra, no underwriter can offer a safeguard against relatives or unscrupulous fortune hunters, and sometimes the relatives *are* the fortune hunters. For example, shortly after it became known that Las Vegas's Kirk Kerkorian had become a one-man, half-billion-dollar conglomerate, he complained: "I never before knew I had so many relatives."

Aristotle Onassis is no different. He helps support at least fifty relatives—sisters, uncles, aunts, and God knows how many cousins, first, second, and third—in the style they feel they should be accustomed to, at a total of over

$125,000 annually. Onassis, with his Greek devotion to the family line, pays willingly if the relatives can establish their blood link to his satisfaction. Though usually easy with a buck, Onassis does balk at being tapped by unrelated charitable organizations which piously claim they are dedicated to the assistance of the afflicted, undernourished, and underprivileged. One of Ari's many secretaries in the United States, says that his employer constantly receives letters expecting him to contribute to every church in the country. In one typical week the postman brought to Mr. Onassis solicitations from the First Presbyterian, the Third Serbian Orthodox, the Church of Christ, Scientist, St. Francis Xavier Chapel, and Temple B'nai Jeshurun.

Mr. Onassis might be pouring untold millions into charitable coffers, but if that is so he has managed to keep it quiet. (Since he pays no income tax, he needs no deductions.) Greek author and journalist Stephanos Zotos says: "During the thirty years I have been writing about Aristotle Onassis, I have yet to hear that he has given as much as a pair of cuff links to charity." There is as yet no Onassis School for Tropical Disease Research, no Onassis Wing at Salonika University, and not even a solitary Onassis Foundation any place. Apparently Ari subscribes to the old adage that no good deed goes unpunished.

It is common knowledge by now that Jackie, besides being a compulsive shopper, is a compulsive redecorator. During her years in the White House she redecorated the living quarters so often—she sometimes changed everything around in the course of a single day—that on occasion the President felt like a stranger when he came upstairs from the executive offices after work. The poor man had to search for his favorite chair and a familiar corner where he could sit down and quietly read his newspaper or ponder the immense cares of state. In his memoirs of the Kennedy administration, Press Secretary Pierre Salinger wrote: "When the Kennedys moved in, so did the carpenters."

The President usually let Jackie tinker, as long as she did not interfere with strict regulations or come up against the various committees that had the authority to preserve the essential "mood" of the Executive Mansion. However, he said a stern "no" to Jackie when she wanted to change the color in the Blue Room, which she detested. President Kennedy felt sure that such an alteration would create a terrible political flap. To bolster his argument against redoing the Blue Room, he reminded Jackie that Dolly Madison had once bought a mirror in Paris for $50 without authorization, and Congress, incensed, had conducted a noisy investigation into the matter that cost $2,800.

A friend of Jackie's once remarked that, if by some miracle, she were given supervision of the Vatican, it wouldn't be twenty-four hours before she'd decide that she didn't like the way things looked in the Sistine Chapel, and she'd start doing the place over.

With Jackie's long record as a redecorator, it is not startling that since she married Mr. Onassis she has been focusing a critical eye on the interiors of all his residences. After they had been married about eight months, she finally convinced herself that it was necessary to redecorate the villa at Glyfada. Never one to do things sparingly—maybe pick up a rug at Macy's and a lamp at Gimbel's—Jackie got on the long-distance telephone to New York and engaged the very elegant interior decorator Billy Baldwin. Mr. Baldwin, who charges an arm and a leg for redecorating as much as a rabbit hutch, has, among his blue-chip clients, Mrs. William Paley and Mrs. Henry Luce.

Mr. Baldwin threw himself entirely into the service of Mrs. Onassis. He made two trips to Greece to look things over. He strolled back and forth through the Glyfada villa with Jackie, while a secretary followed the pair, making notes on what was to stay, and what was to go. By the time Mr. Baldwin—who gets a commission on everything purchased—was finished, mighty little was to stay. After he won Jackie's agreement for his "master plan," Mr. Baldwin started purchasing discreetly in New York, London, and Paris.

When Mr. Baldwin accepts a commission, he guards the privacy of his client with his honor. But interior decorators have buzzing about them, in their private lives and in their employ, young men and women who drink cocktails in the "singles" and "gay" bars on New York's Second and Third Avenues and thereabouts, as well as in their European counterparts, and who chatter like magpies. So gradually the stupendous sums being lavished in Glyfada became the talk of the trade.

I picked up a tip here and there, and finally I nailed down Mr. David Barrett, a New York importer of classic pieces, and Mr. Barrett admitted: "Yes, Mr. Baldwin bought a number of superior tables from me—$10,000 worth—and because Mrs. Onassis was in a hurry, I had to crate them and ship them to Athens by air."

Thomas d'Angelis, another expensive New York furniture dealer, who sells only through decorators, confirmed a private report that his firm had also done a "pleasing" amount of business with Mrs. Onassis, through the good offices of Billy Baldwin. D'Angelis acknowledged that he

had air-shipped to Glyfada fifteen contemporary chairs
and sofas. These fifteen items cost $10,000 for the basic
frames, plus $12,000 for upholstery to cover them, a total
of $22,000. Those of us who must of necessity buy Castro
convertibles on the monthly-payment plan should note
that each one of Mr. d'Angelis' precious chairs and sofas
cost $1,466, and they are among the *cheapest* items bought
for Glyfada.

I sought the advice of one of New York's most highly
respected interior decorators, who for thirty-five years has
been doing some of the grandest homes in New York,
Palm Beach, Palm Springs, and Nassau. He concluded
that, considering Mrs. Onassis' and Mr. Baldwin's rich
tastes, redoing Glyfada will cost between $750,000 and
$1,250,000.

There appears to be another reason, besides her compulsive desire to change things around, that motivated
Jackie to order Glyfada done over from top to bottom.
When Jackie moved in, Glyfada was full of items bought
by Maria Callas, and these things *had* to go. Mrs. Naya
Tolischus, the Greek widow of the New York *Times*'s
Pulitzer Prize-winning correspondent Otto Tolischus,
who used to own the Glyfada villa, told me: "I sold the
villa, which I had owned for many years, to Mr. Onassis
in 1962. He said, at the time, that he was buying it for
the use of Maria Callas. He and Miss Callas occupied it,
on and off, until May, 1968, when Mr. Onassis and Mrs.
Kennedy decided to get married."

Upon being told of the impending Onassis-Kennedy
nuptials, Miss Callas moved out of Glyfada in what can
best be described as blind fury, accompanied by light-
ning, thunder, and winds of hurricane force. She cried:

"First I lost my weight. Then I lost my voice. Now I've lost Onassis."

Glyfada isn't the only redecorating job that currently engages Mrs. Onassis. She has a still bigger project on Skorpios, where she is building an entirely new villa, again putting her ideas together with Mr. Baldwin's. Interviewed in Athens, Costas Harritakis, the city's most eminent antique dealer, said: "Jackie has undertaken to purchase furniture and decorations for the villa at Skorpios with a special preference for French rustic style. She has been dropping in every week and purchasing more and more things." The Skorpios job will probably come to $1,600,000 or so.

Ari doesn't always agree with Jackie on just what should go into their various homes. Mr. Baldwin, for once breaking his vow of silence, simply could not resist telling friends what happened when Ari and Jackie had a difference, in his presence, over the furnishings for the villa at Skorpios. Jackie, said Mr. Baldwin, made her preference known by "standing behind Onassis' back and making a little face."

Now, let's get down to cases on that incredible figure of $20,000,000 per year—and, when we do, we see that it all really does add up. Here are the dollars and cents of the matter, the information having been gleaned by my small network of spies and the statistics put together for me by a senior accountant in one of the nation's top firms.

WHERE DID ALL THE MONEY GO?

*An accounting of
what Mr. and Mrs. Aristotle Onassis spent
during their first year of marriage*

WEDDING
Transport of guests to Skorpios Island from
three continents for nuptials; their lodging
in Athens; post-wedding party aboard yacht
Christina; imported foodstuffs, wines; flowers; orchestra; entertainment $40,500

HOMES
Rent of apartments and hotel suites in
New York and London; maintenance of
apartments and homes in Paris, Monte
Carlo, Glyfada, on Skorpios Island, and in
Montevideo, Uruguay $1,985,000
Construction and furnishing of new villa
on Skorpios $1,600,000
Complete redecoration and refurnishing of
villa at Glyfada $1,050,000

SERVANTS
Salaries for 202 full-time help—domestics,
chefs, gardeners, chauffeurs, social secretaries, etc., in the U.S., Europe, and South
America $727,200
Food, lodging, and unemployment insur-
ance for 202 servants, plus their families $303,000
Other expenses relating to servants: fringe
benefits, medical care, pregnancies, Social
Security, pensions, funerals, (including an
estimate of what they steal) $363,600

SECURITY
Fees and maintenance of round-the-clock
guards at homes in Greece; also Jackie's
and Ari's personal bodyguards while traveling and while staying in New York, Paris,
and London $84,000

YACHT
Upkeep of *Christina* $1,140,000

JEWELRY
Ari's gifts to Jackie . . . (Brace yourself) $5,000,000

ART
Paintings, sculptures, precious china, other
artifacts $887,000

JACKIE'S PERSONAL EXPENSES
Her dresses, furs, cosmetics and cosmetic
care, "minor" jewelry, her gifts to others $1,250,000

ARI'S PERSONAL EXPENSES
His clothes, personal barber, out-of-pocket
tips, cash handouts, etc. $19,500

CHILDREN
Alexander Onassis' allowance $100,000
Christina Onassis' allowance $75,000
Caroline and John Kennedy's allowances,
tuitions, governesses, clothes, general up-
keep $30,000

ARI'S RELATIVES
All fifty of them .... $ 25,000

ARI'S GIFTS TO OTHERS BESIDES
JACKIE
Including addition of $1,000,000 to his chil-
dren's trust fund, gift to Maria Callas of
$50,000, gifts of jewelry and other valuables
to friends and relatives $1,118,000

AUTOMOBILES
Maintenance of twelve automobiles (in-
cluding three Rolls-Royces) in France,
Greece, and Uruguay $13,400
Rental of chauffered limousines—one for
Ari, one for Jackie—in New York, London,
or elsewhere, at horrendous daily rates $16,200

ENTERTAINING AT HOME AND DINING OUT

Maintaining guests at their various homes and aboard the *Christina;* parties; guides, extra cars, chauffeurs; special chefs, foodstuffs, wines; musicians, entertainers $105,000
Restaurants and nightclubs for Ari and Jackie and their endless (non-business-related) parties with large numbers of guests @ $1,650 a week $85,860

TRAVEL

For Mr. and Mrs. Onassis, their relatives (excluding children), guests, secretaries, bodyguards, personal maids, and valets; fares and other expenses of transportation; hotels, gratuities, sightseeing. (This item does not include the cost of traveling on the *Christina.*) $178,000

MEDICAL

Doctors and medicine, including full-time physician in Greece $22,000

INSURANCE

All types of insurance for Jackie, Ari, the children, and their personal belongings—homes, jewels, art, yacht $1,906,000

TAXES

Land, highway, water, school, and other taxes, directly related to their various homes $2,000,000
Jackie's Federal, New York State, and New York City income taxes, and her other U.S. taxes. (Ari pays no income tax in the U.S. or anywhere else.) $72,000

MISCELLANEOUS
Even a billionaire loses some small change
he can't account for. He gets a hole in his
pocket, and a few dimes and pennies and
drachmas trickle through a subway grating $20,000

TOTAL $20,316,260

Chapter Six

DIAMONDS ARE A GIRL'S BEST FRIEND

Several hours after Jackie was married to Mr. Onassis, a few intimate friends and relatives of the bride and groom were cutting up at a wedding party on the good yacht *Christina*, docked at Skorpios. The music was being pumped out fiercely by a tuxedoed Greek band—everything from the Greek national anthem to *Blue Suede Shoes*, an old Elvis Presley hit that Jackie digs. Toasts were being exchanged in English, Greek, and French, everybody was God-blessing everybody else, and Ari had the first dance with Jackie.

One of those present was Mrs. Theodore Garoufalidis, Ari's sister (they're very close), who, a few days later, told her teatime pals in Athens all about the bash, and particularly about the high point of the evening. "Everybody was dancing and talking and being very merry," said Mrs. Garoufalidis, "when Jackie asked the drummer to beat a flourish, and when she had everyone's attention she said: 'Would you like to see what Ari gave me?' Suddenly it was as quiet as a tomb. We were all dying with curiosity. Ari sat back, smiling like a cat who had just swallowed a canary. Jackie went below and when she returned she was wearing a new diamond ring—so heavy, my God, I don't know how she could hold her hand up—and a bracelet, a necklace, and two absolutely incredible pendants made of diamonds and rubies, rubies maybe big as strawberries."

Jackie's mother, Janet Auchincloss, who herself has an overstuffed jewel box back in Newport and is something of an expert on precious stones, stood up and closely examined the jewels on her daughter who had made good. Mrs. Auchincloss could scarcely believe her eyes. A king's ransom, indeed! Jackie, exquisitely happy, took off the ring and handed it over to Janet Auchincloss, who, in turn, let her granddaughter, Caroline Kennedy, hold it in her hand. Suddenly, all the guests assembled felt faint as the child tossed the ring up in the air.

Nobody was forgotten that wedding night. Ari presented zodiac rings to Lee Radziwell, Jean Smith, and Pat Lawford, *and* to the awed Mrs. Auchincloss. Caroline received a gold bracelet with semiprecious stones, which she wore the next day while donkey riding, and John got an Accutron watch, which he promptly tried to wind, then to feed to the cat.

A few days later, the jewels Ari gave Jackie as wedding presents were estimated by jewelers in several countries, whose opinions were solicited, to be worth a healthy $1,000,000. When these figures were printed, Mrs. Auchincloss was back in New York, and Pittsburgh's "Bunny"

Mellon said to her: "Dear Janet, you haven't lost a daughter—you've gained a diamond mine!"

Ari's wedding offerings to his new goddess was just the beginning of a shower of gems that reminded Greek scholars of the Golden Age of Pericles. Since the wedding, so the story goes in the close-knit international jewelry fraternity, Jackie has received from her husband, one of the last of the big diamond buyers, another $4,000,000 worth of beautiful baubles, bringing his jewelry bill, during their first year of togetherness, up to $5,000,000.

One night, to celebrate Jackie's fortieth birthday, Ari hosted a party at the Neraida night club in Palaion Phaleron, a seaside suburb ten miles from Athens. When Jackie arrived she startled everybody in the club, as she had startled the guests on the *Christina* ten months before, by wearing what amounted to an entire display window of new jewels. Ari's birthday gifts, what else? They included a solid gold belt with Jackie's astrological sign, the head of a lion. Also swinging from Jackie's earlobes, like a couple of Ping-Pong balls, was a pair of "Apollo 11" earrings to commemorate the first walk on the moon.

At the party Katina Paxinou, the Greek stage star, was seated alongside Mrs. Onassis, and when she complimented Jackie on her earrings, Jackie laughed and said: "Ari was actually apologetic about them. He felt they were kind of bargain-basement trinkets. But he promised me that, if I'm good, next year he'll give me the moon itself." (A different version of this incident has it that the earrings were a gift; not from Ari, but from Zolotas, the jeweler.)

But the main attraction of the birthday evening was Jackie's new ring. It has a forty-carat diamond—a diamond, as Scott Fitzgerald would have said, as big as the Ritz. Ilias Lalaounis, jewelry designer and manager of the Zolotas jewelry store, told Costas Skouras, this writer's assistant in Greece, that Jackie's latest and greatest diamond was probably purchased in London (Onassis is closemouthed about such things) and is worth between $600,000 and $1,000,000. A New York jeweler appraised it at a "flat million."

Jackie's birthday trinkets are not the sort of things one picks up ready-made, not even on the counters of such considerable establishments as Tiffany's or Cartier's. They must be made to order, by a master craftsman. The moon earrings, for example, were made by Lalaounis, who worked on them for over a month on instructions given by Onassis himself, who kept dropping in, from time to time, to see how the $150,000 trinket was coming along. When asked later what would have happened if the moon walk had been canceled, Lalaounis merely shrugged. He described the earrings thus: "Their eighteen-carat gold clasp fits the ear with a small globe representing the earth. The globe is set with sapphires and diamonds. From this globe depart four spacecraft that form the golden chain that links the earth with the moon. It is a true replica of the pictures issued by NASA of the moon, and is covered with rubies and diamonds."

Among those who enjoyed Onassis' hospitality at the Neraida were six detectives. The check for dinner was 10,000 drachmas—$330—before tips. Ari usually tips a hundred percent of the check, plus wads of currency to the orchestra for playing Jackie's favorite tunes.

Ari has been far more generous with Jackie than he was with his first wife, Tina Livanos Onassis. When Ari and Tina were divorced after ten years of marriage, it was stated in court that Tina's jewels were worth only $4,000,000.

Jackie's primary wedding and birthday gifts are both what Harry Winston, a New York society jeweler, defines as "important pieces." An "important piece," according to Mr. Winston, is "a jewel or collection of jewels that kills every other piece within twenty feet." When Jackie wears her forty-carat diamond ring in Athens it does more than "kill" every other piece in the neighborhood. Its impact is felt south to Saudi Arabia and north to Lapland, and in that wide area every other woman of means regards her own jewels as little better than glass beads from Woolworth's.

Everybody in New York jet-set circles is now wondering what Ari will give Jackie next. The Eiffel Tower? The Empire State Building? The Taj Mahal? Angkor Wat?

Besides the jewelry he has given Jackie, he has apparently given her carte-blanche authority to pick up any knickknacks here and there that catch her fancy. Jackie has done just that, in New York, London, Paris, Rome, and Athens, and, in addition to buying ready-mades, she's helped create some of her own pieces, particularly with the aid of David Webb, the brilliant young New York jewelry designer. Discussing his famous client, Webb told me: "Mrs. Onassis has high, expensive style. She knows what she wants. She is very determined and ingenious."

David Webb's recent bills to Mrs. Onassis came to $60,000. Dealing with Webb, she always presents the original idea. For example, one time she wanted an exotic Indian-style pair of earrings. Webb, working with his precision tools in his East 57th Street studio, made the earrings with rubies, emeralds, and pearls. They're as Indian-looking as Bombay. On another occasion, Mr. Webb made for Jackie a necklace with rubies and diamonds.

Jackie's curious friends are shattered because she has never, on her many visits to New York, brought with her any of the important pieces Ari bought her; they have been dying to see them. Well, if they want to see the jewels, they'll have to go to Greece, because Jackie is still an American citizen, even though her husband is Greek-Argentinian, and the customs duties on, say, $5,000,000 in gems would be horrendous—roughly twenty-four percent, or nearly $1,200,000, according to New York customs officials.

Jackie is doing more and more of her jewelry buying in foreign currencies. On one of her Mediterranean cruises, the *Christina* stopped over at Capri for one shopping day. Jackie zoomed into Campanina's jewelry store, and just as fast as you can fill your shopping cart at the corner supermarket, she spent $10,000. Campanina's was elated as Jackie selected white enamel jewelry, knickknacks, earrings, cuff links, a star-studded pin, and earrings—yes, more earrings. One reporter, Helen Dudar, said that Jackie was buying "at least two of everything she doesn't buy four of. It's hard to imagine her wearing anything that is not this year's fashion, except possibly last year's jewelry."

While the U.S. Customs would love to get its hands on Jackie's foreign-bought gems, so would any respectable jewel thief. Most of the time Jackie's riches repose in a safe deposit vault, or are watched by armed guards. But despite all caution, jewels such as Jackie's are relatively easy to steal, if the culprit involved is willing to risk being severely ventilated. A clue to what the insurance companies think of the risk of wearing such valuable items on one's finger, neck, or earlobes is given in the case of Mrs. Harriet Annenberg Ames, who is the sister of Walter Annenberg, U.S. Ambassador to Great Britain. Mrs. Ames owned the sixty-three-carat diamond ring that was purchased, in the fall of 1969, by Richard Burton, who also declares his love in millions, for his wife, Elizabeth Taylor. After the sale, Mrs. Ames sighed and said she was glad to be rid of that ring because, even for a woman of her vast means, the insurance was prohibitive. She figured out that each time she took the diamond out of her safe deposit vault and wore it, it cost her $1,500 in insurance premiums. Being of a frugal bent, Mrs. Ames allowed herself the luxury of donning it only twenty times in 1968, thus reducing her premiums to $30,000 for the year. It can be assumed that it costs Jackie Onassis six or seven times that amount in insurance every time she appears in public with the loot Ari has bestowed upon her.

Jackie's jewels give the insurance people palpitations, not only because they're choice targets for burglars but also because Jackie handles them so carelessly. Consider the diamond wedding ring Caroline played ball with. One time, when the *Christina* was docked at Skorpios, she simply could not find the ring. It was lost. Now, Mr. Onassis, for all his wealth, is never one to take such a mishap lightly. He sent the crew of the *Christina* ashore to search every inch of the areas of Skorpios where Jackie had recently been. And he and Jackie and the domestic servants began a stateroom-by-stateroom, nook-and-cranny search of the yacht itself.

After a couple of hours Jackie, exhausted from opening

and closing drawers and looking behind vases and under the sofa cushions, was in tears, but Mr. Onassis, ever the hunter, pressed on. Three hysterical hours later the ring was found by a housekeeper—under a rug.

God knows how it got there, but there are many theories, all of them revolving around Jackie's habit of constantly taking off the ring, and other pieces of jewelry, for no good reason, or just to let the curious hold, if ever so briefly, such treasures. In this Jackie is similar to Elizabeth Taylor Burton, who is credited with having a $5,000,000 jewelry collection. One of Mrs. Burton's favorites is a classic large pearl, and this has vanished three times since her husband bought it for her. The first time was when the couple was staying in a Las Vegas hotel. "Elizabeth only had it a week," recalls Richard Burton, "when it disappeared completely. . . . Elizabeth, knowing I was in a bad mood, was afraid to tell me she'd lost the pearl. Then one day, one of the Pekes was chewing on what she thought was a bone in the corner. It turned out to be the pearl, and the dog's teeth marks are still on it."

Another woman of vast fortune who was notoriously absent-minded about her valuables was Arabella Huntington, widow of Collis P. Huntington of the Southern Pacific Railroad. One afternoon, after looking at some furniture in the antiques firm of French & Company in New York, Mrs. Huntington departed, leaving behind on a desk a handbag containing eleven pearl necklaces valued at $3,500,000. (*Now* do you know why the executives of firms that insure jewelry are given to nervous tics and bleeding ulcers?)

Jackie's on-and-off bit with her jewels was witnessed by an enthralled audience one June night in 1969 when she and Ari, in one of their first American public appearances since their marriage, went to the Metropolitan Opera House in New York to see the Royal Ballet. During the performance, it seemed that as many people were watching the Onassises through opera glasses, as were watching the onstage leaps and jumps of Dame Margot Fonteyn and Rudi Nureyev. What magnetized the ladies present was Jackie's astonishingly large emerald-and-diamond earrings. At one point the house went momentarily pitch black, and when normal lighting was resumed people could be heard whispering: "She's taken them off!"

After the ballet, Jackie and Ari went to a party at the town house of Mr. Ronald Tree, for food and drink and small talk with the likes of Mrs. Vincent Astor and columnist Joseph Alsop. At the Trees's, Jackie reached into her purse and put the earrings back on. No explanation for this unusual conduct was given, but students of "important" jewels came up with a precedent that perhaps solved the riddle. It seems that during the Deauville season in 1965 the most famous earrings were the diamond pendants owned by Mrs. Eric Loder, said to cost $1,000,-000 in hard cash. According to an eyewitness, Mrs. Loder's earrings "were big as teaspoons, and because of their weight and the consequent strain of wearing them, she detached them, at intervals during the evening, to give her ears a rest."

While Ari likes to see Jackie in any of her many earrings, rings, clasps, or golden stomachers, his favorite type of jewel is the bracelet.

Chapter Seven

BRACELETS FOR BREAKFAST

The Aegean Sea sparkles with the beauty of a summer morning. A messenger carrying a flower box leaves the jewelry shop of E. Zolotas, 6 University Place, in the chic, leafy heart of Athens and motors nineteen miles to the coastal town of Glyfada. There he leaves the flower box at the delivery entrance of a sumptuous villa overlooking the sea.

Domestics put the contents of the flower box in a graceful silver vase, and put the vase on a tray, and deliver the tray, along with breakfast, to the bedroom occupied by Mrs. Aristotle Socrates Onassis.

Mrs. Onassis reaches into the bunched flowers expectantly, as if on a treasure hunt, for she knows from long experience that some kind of a treat awaits her. On this morning it is a diamond-studded bracelet!

77

The story behind the bracelet and flowers, one worthy of Hans Christian Anderson, was explained by Ilias Lalaounis, manager of the Zolotas shop.

"In May, 1968," said Lalaounis, "Mr. Onassis called here and asked us to send to Jackie every two weeks a bouquet of flowers with a golden or diamond-studded bracelet. I am sure Mrs. Onassis must have by now a small museum of the Zolotas firm. She must have at least thirty bracelets."

Each bracelet costs 70,000 drachmas, or $2,300—a total of $69,000. Zolotas does not charge for the flowers.

It is Jackie's custom always to sleep in a room separate from her husband's. Ever conscious of her appearance, she will never admit her husband until she is fully awake, has had her coffee, and is ready to face the world. Maude Shaw, Caroline Kennedy's governess in the White House, once made a remark that quickly circulated among the Presidential staff. "Mrs. Kennedy would no more see her husband," said Miss Shaw, "until she fixed her hair and her face than Queen Elizabeth would receive the Prime Minister wearing her bathrobe."

Onassis, who besides being the most lavish, might also be the most attentive husband around, makes his presence felt each morning, even if he's in Tibet, by having something placed on Jackie's tray. Of course, it's not always a bracelet. A bracelet a day would be a bore. Sometimes, if he's away, it might be a poem proclaiming his affections, sent by overnight cable. These poems, according to those who have seen them, do not place Onassis in T. S. Eliot's class, nor even, for that matter, in Georgie Jessel's.

One time, when Onassis was secretly in Tokyo on a deal involving tanker construction, Jackie, who was in New York, found on her tray one of Mikimoto's finest strings of cultured pearls—wound around a roll. The necklace had been flown halfway around the world by air express, addressed to one of Onassis' assistants, with instructions on exactly how it should be presented to his wife.

Even when Mr. Onassis is in the next room, the breakfast tray has a surprise. According to a talkative crew member of the *Christina,* it is sometimes a formal social invitation like this:

> *Mr. Aristotle Onassis requests the pleasure of your company for deck tennis at 11:30 A.M. aboard the motor ship* Christina.

This, it must be admitted, is somewhat corny. But what American wife would not be delighted with such persistent attention, even if her husband were not one of the richest men in the world?

It should be remembered, when talking about Jackie's jewels, that even before she married Mr. Onassis she had a collection that would have delighted ninety-nine percent of the female population. John Kennedy gave her, besides a diamond wedding ring, an emerald engagement ring and a whale of a thick Tiffany bracelet. And that wasn't all. Jackie often wore in her hair a $7,000 sunburst clip.

During the Kennedy years in the White House, when, with the Secret Service ever present, there was no fret about thieves, Jackie kept all her jewels in her suite in three large cases. She was constantly taking them out and polishing them and putting them back in and changing them around from case to case. The idea of all this shifting, it was explained, was to have each case hold the proper jewels for wearing on different occasions.

That is, one held the daytime—luncheon and tea—ornaments. The second held evening, but not necessarily formal, jewels. And the third held sparklers for very formal occasions—state dinners, royal receptions, things like that. You can just imagine how mortified a girl like Jacqueline Onassis would be to be discovered wearing, at a white-tie Buckingham Palace dinner, a diamond that one would wear having lunch with the girls at the drugstore counter.

Jackie acquired some jewels as First Lady that became controversial, to say the least. In years past, most First Ladies usually regarded any valuable gift from a foreign government or head of state as being the property of the United States, nothing personal at all. Mrs. Roosevelt, and other First Ladies, usually would donate any highly priced gewgaws to museums, or hold them for an eventual collection of their husband's papers and souvenirs, like the Eisenhower collection at Gettysburg and the Truman museum at Independence, Missouri.

Jackie couldn't quite see it that way. She, with her love of life, couldn't bring herself to commit "living" jewelry to "dead" museums.

When President Ayub Khan visited the Executive Mansion he presented Mrs. Kennedy with a ruby, turquoise, and diamond necklace, reportedly costing $100,000, which she promptly popped into one of her cases, the "superformal" one. She also kept a gold, ruby, diamond, and pearl belt presented to her by King Hassan II of Morocco. And she adores the nifty wafer-thin Cartier watch presented by the City Council of Paris. (You can read the time on this watch, if you're not blinded by its sparkling diamonds.)

Mary Barelli Gallagher stirred up this "private vs.

public" acceptance of foreigners' jeweled offerings to the First Lady when she reported that Jackie tried, without success, to have some stupendous jewels removed, for her personal use, from a ceremonial sword presented to the President by the King of Saudi Arabia. (A sniffing dowager, commenting on Jackie's attitude toward such gifts, said: "If Jacqueline's standards prevail, someday a President of the United States, when his time in office ends, will take with him into private life an aircraft carrier.")

It would be erroneous to believe that when Aristotle Onassis goes out and plunks down $1,000,000 to buy Jackie a little ring for her finger, or $50,000 for a new painting to cover a crack in the wall of their villa at Glyfada, he's throwing money away like a bombed sailor. Good diamonds and good paintings have proved to be, since World War II, a far better investment than the stock market.

J. Paul Getty, who first alerted his buddy Onassis on this matter, has long been saying to his friends—and to the readers of *Playboy* magazine—that fine art is the *finest* investment. "The dollars and cents value of paintings, sculpture, tapestries, fine antique furniture, and practically all forms of art," said Mr. Getty, "have shown a marked tendency to rise—and even soar—over the years."

Mr. Getty offers one goggling example: Paul Gauguin's *Te tiai Na Oe i te Rata*—"Do You Await a Letter?"—which is said to have been sold for less than $50. At an auction in 1959, the painting realized more than $300,000. Mr. Getty really doesn't have to go outside of his own personal experience to make his point. "About twenty-five years ago," he said, "I attended an art sale at Sotheby's in London. Among the objects on sale was a rather battered Italian painting of a Madonna—a work, the Sotheby experts declared, produced by some unknown artist. Although the Madonna was badly begrimed and in a poor state of preservation, I liked the picture; it was, I thought, reminiscent of Raphael. I bought it—for $200.

"In 1963, I decided to have the painting cleaned. The job was entrusted to the famous firm of restorers, Thomas Agnew & Sons. Representatives of the firm soon called me excitedly. The painting was, indeed, the work of Raphael, they said—and this was quickly authenticated by art experts. . . . The painting I purchased for $200 has proved to be Raphael's *Madonna di Loreto*, painted in 1508-1509. Its real value—upwards of a million dollars."

What's true of painting is also true of jewels. In 1957 Stavros Niarchos purchased for his then wife Eugenie, who died in 1970, a 130-carat pear-shaped diamond with a (roughly) $1,000,000 price tag on it. It is now estimated that this rock could be sold, on the open market, for two and one half times what it cost Mr. Niarchos. Another recent example is the diamond Richard Burton purchased for his Elizabeth in 1969 from Tiffany's for $1,150,000. This gem was purchased only ten year before by Mrs. Harriet Annenberg Ames for $550,000.

Most of the millions that Mr. and Mrs. Onassis spend, outside of the food they consume, and the dresses that go out of fashion, and the servants who have no resale value, is a form of equity. "If Mr. Onassis is a billionaire today," wrote one of the editors of the London *Times* financial pages, "he will eventually be a double billionaire, merely by doing nothing, just holding on to his properties and living long enough."

Ari's El Greco, if auctioned today in New York or London, would net him a half-million-dollar profit. His collection of ancient Greek artifacts would bring him $200,000-plus over what he paid for them.

When the average Joe zips open his purse and "invests" in a diamond or painting, hoping that it can in good time be resold for a profit, he's taking an awful chance. The jewelry and art business is acrawl with phonies. But the Gettys and the Niarchoses and the Onassises seldom get taken; they consult experts.

One time an Italian dealer tried to peddle Mr. Onassis a "genuine Michelangelo" on which the paint was barely dry. And Paul Getty recalls that one man tried to sell him what he said was a rare sixteenth-century tapestry, and for a "mere $45,000." When Mr. Getty said he wasn't interested, the man flew into a rage. "But you've *got* to buy it!" he shouted. "My wife worked months to make it."

Well, it all comes down to this: When you see Jackie Onassis walking around loaded with "important" pieces, remember that she's also wearing important investments. But hasn't this always been so? The rich get richer and the poor read all about it in the society pages.

Unfortunately, John Kennedy could never see Jackie as an "investor." Her hunger for ever more jewels and clothes—particularly clothes—kept him in an everlasting stew.

Chapter Eight

THE COMPULSIVE SHOPPER

In March of 1963, John Kennedy was deep in crisis. The situation in Vietnam was going downhill. Saigon was crying for more American aid. A new incident in Berlin threatened another U.S.-Soviet confrontation. And the civil rights movement in the South was accompanied by riot and murder.

The President was badly in need of a piece of good news, and it came, one day, from an unexpected source. He was shown a financial statement to the effect that for January and February of 1963, his wife had spent *only* $16,000 on herself. In the same period, during 1962, she had spent $28,000, a considerable portion of which was for clothes. All the members of the White House staff quickly learned of these figures, and how delighted the President was.

The staff was aware of something that the President, with all his other frightful responsibilities, had apparently overlooked. But they did not intend to tell him what it was, for it would have robbed him of his needed moment of joy. The President had not realized the reason that Mrs. Kennedy's expenses had dropped, for the two-month period, was that she was pregnant, fulfilling few social obligations, spending lots of time in seclusion, and thus doing a minimum amount of shopping.

For many months before that time it had been gossiped about that the President and Jackie had been at each other's throats because her personal expenditures were running wild. This troubled John Kennedy not only because of the drain on his pocketbook, but because the press was kicking it around and the publicity was a political liability. Jackie herself tried to quash some of the reports, but when she did her remarks only served to give the matter more attention. When it was reported that she had spent $50,000 on clothes during her first fifteen months as the First Lady, Jackie stated publicly: "I couldn't spend that much unless I wore sable underwear." Naturally, this crack made a nifty headline.

Newspaper speculation about Jackie's expenses, sometimes right, sometimes wrong, began well before Mr. Kennedy was elected. At the height of the Nixon-Kennedy campaign, in 1960, when Mrs. Nixon was sporting her famous bargain-store cloth coat, it was reported that Mrs. Kennedy had bought heavily in Paris at the elegant houses of Cardin, Grès, Chanel, and Balenciaga. These masters of dress design, it was pointed out, charge roughly $1,500 for a simple tailored suit, and a Balenciaga ball gown is about $2,000. Furthermore, the fashion pages revealed that with the sleeveless linen dresses that the

First Lady favored, she wore colored enamel gold bangles from Tiffany's that were priced from $1,225 to $3,450, and these were said to be but minor trinkets in her "secondary jewelry collection."

Jackie's spending, and the ensuing news coverage, drove Pierre Salinger, the Presidential press secretary, to distraction. Jackie realized Mr. Salinger's problems and gave him a photograph of herself inscribed, in her schoolgirl scrawl: "From the cross you have to bear."

The President, usually diplomatic with press lords, lost his cool over Jackie's spending. John Fairchild, publisher of *Women's Wear Daily*, the trade paper of the clothing industry, recalled what happened to him at the time: "I received a call from the White House," said Mr. Fairchild. "It was Pierre Salinger on the phone. He told me the President was displeased with all the stories about Mrs. Kennedy's clothes."

The President would rage every time Jackie made one of her well-publicized trips to New York to go shopping. She stayed at the elegant Carlyle Hotel, and there, before ever-watchful reporters camped in the lobby, passed a parade of dress designers to show Mrs. Kennedy their latest creations. They were invariably accompanied by young men heavily burdened with packages and by models who were Jackie's size.

Not only was Mrs. Kennedy a blessing to interior decorators, dress designers, hairdressers, and milliners, but she often included them in her luncheon and theater parties and visits to discothèques. On one visit to New York, a photographer got a candid shot of her dancing with an effeminate clothes creator. When the President met Jackie on her return to the White House, he promptly said: "For God's sake, Jackie! Can't you steer clear of the Nellie boys until I'm re-elected?"

Certainly the President had his re-election in 1964 constantly on his mind, and that was the reason he was so often shocked by Jackie's out-of-sight appearance. He was cautioned by one of his political cronies in the "Irish Mafia" that one of Jackie's "stuck-up" gowns could cost him Tennessee, maybe even Kentucky as well.

Her kookie hairdos also had Mr. Kennedy climbing the wall. Like the day before Jackie was going off to Europe on a private visit and her favorite hairdresser, Kenneth, came to the White House from his New York salon to fix Mrs. Kennedy's hair in her third-floor sitting room. He gave her his famous "restless and savage" cut, which was, at the time, the trademark of the international jet set, a trademark John Kennedy was most anxious to avoid.

When the President saw Jackie's new coiffure he whistled. He asked Kenneth to please tone it down, it would make every aging female in the Midwest uptight. Later, Pierre Salinger recalled that the President, smiling, had said to Kenneth: "Say, are *you* trying to make sure I won't get re-elected?"

In New York, Jackie often went (and still goes) to Kenneth's five-story building on East 54th Street, which has, among other things, nine hundred yards of Indian jungle-flower carpeting, made by Scotland's master weavers. Kenneth charges $10 for a shampoo and set, and $25 or $30 for a personal haircut. Kenneth's clients have graced thousands of magazine covers; great faces, like the late Marilyn Monroe, Barbara Streisand, and Lee Radziwill. Lee once said: "Kenneth won't put his hands in your hair unless you're famous—or have thirty dollars."

John Kennedy finally was willing to settle for one thing. Jackie could continue to have her cosmetic and sartorial adventures, if she would only, for God's sake, be reasonable and limit herself, say, to spending $1,000 a week. Was that asking too much? But Jackie couldn't control herself. A glittering clasp, or a smart scarf sitting in a display window, almost hypnotizes her. And then—*pow!*—she's in that store and ordering and ordering.

Discussing her sister's rich tastes, and the President's futile efforts to budget them, Lee once said: "Trying to make Jackie Kennedy stick to a budget is as ridiculous as trying to make Dean Martin stick to milk."

Jackie was inclined to treat the President's frustrations lightly. One day early in 1963 she came to New York from Washington and, lunching with friends at La Caravelle, said: "Sometimes the President seems more concerned with my budget than with the budget of the United States."

Jackie did not curtail her New York sorties, and one evening this caused a sticky situation. There was a reception at the White House for Secretary of State Dean Rusk, and as the honorable personages assembled, the word was passed that, unfortunately, Mrs. Kennedy would not be in attendance. She was "indisposed." When one European Ambassador shook hands with the President, the Ambassador conveyed to Mr. Kennedy his regrets that the First Lady was "under the weather," and he wished her a speedy recovery.

When the President was out of earshot, the Ambassador's alert wife asked her husband? "How is it, if Mrs. Kennedy is 'under the weather,' that I heard on the radio just one hour ago that she is in New York being fitted for a new gown by Mr. Cassini?"

Some months later, the President was particularly upset by a trip Jackie made to India. He had stressed to her
the importance of *not* making a big thing about clothes in
that country with its grinding poverty. And so he was
hardly delighted when he saw, on the evening TV news,
the day of her departure, a film of his wife's huge steamer
trunks going aboard a Pan American Airways jet. Nor
was he elated when the television reporter said the
clothes she had with her included previously unworn
gowns from the most expensive houses—Chez Ninon,
Lanvin, Castillo, and Cassini. In closing, the TV reporter
said that Mrs. Kennedy's entourage included her personal
maid and a hairdresser. At that moment President Kennedy must have felt about the television industry the way
Vice President Agnew felt some years later.

In the White House press office, where foreign clippings that might interest the President were assembled,
it was decided that it might be wise not to pass along
to him some of the stories in the Indian left-wing press,
which made anti-American symbols out of Mrs. Kennedy's
Somali leopard coat and her smart mink sweater.

However, he got the dismal tidings from his friend
John Kenneth Galbraith, who was then our Ambassador
in New Delhi. Mr. Galbraith accompanied Jackie around
the country, and wrote in his day-to-day diaries: "I am
having a signal lack of success in soft-pedaling emphasis
on Jackie's clothes. Indeed, cabling a general account of
the journey to the President, I said this effort promised to
be the biggest failure since Stassen tried to ditch Nixon.

"One of the minor footnotes of the trip was some shopping in Benares. . . . J. B. K. hastily bought some silk brocade and a couple of jeweled brocade bags. . . . The papers
made something of the fact that she had spent $600 in

less than five minutes. Actually, it couldn't have been more than ten *seconds*."

It is impossible to keep Presidential family affairs quiet, and one day at the White House mess, the luncheon entertainment concerned the story of how the President had walked into Jacqueline Kennedy's suite without warning and nearly became violent when he saw carpenters enlarging his wife's overflowing clothes closet.

"Jackie," snapped the President, "at this rate you're going to need the Pentagon for your wardrobe."

During one typical year in the White House, Jackie's personal expenditures reached $125,000, or more than her husband earned as President of the United States. So it is not difficult to appreciate that, as the wife of Aristotle Onassis, the twentieth century's Midas, Jackie's personal expenses during their first year of marriage came to ten times that much: $1,250,000-plus. Of course, Onassis can afford it. By his standards the Kennedy's are just scraping along. (Mr. Onassis' own expenses, for his clothes, his personal barber, out-of-pocket tips and cash handouts to the pleading indigent come to $19,500 a year.)

Probably Jackie is now spending more on herself than any other woman in the world, and that includes such extravagant ladies as the wife of the Shah of Persia, Mrs. William Paley, and Elizabeth Taylor, whose husband, Richard Burton, recently said: "Liz can spend $1,000 a minute, and I'm not joking."

In New York in the spring of 1969, Jackie had her finest hours as a speed shopper. She was in and out of dress designers' studios and the smart East Side shops and boutiques so often that *Women's Wear Daily* labeled her "the retailer's best friend," and said: "Jackie Onassis continues to fill her bottomless closets. She is making Daddy O's bills bigger than ever with her latest shopping spree. She is buying in carload lots."

Among Mrs. Onassis' acquisitions during those frenzied weeks were several dresses from Adolfo's. One, an old-fashioned gingham gown, cut something like an apron, was priced at $1,250. Another, a floor-length affair in navy blue with a red border, to be worn over a leotard, was a steal at $400. From Veneziano's Jackie acquired a cotton print jersey shirt, striped cotton pants, and white thonged sandles, also two pairs of buckled, brown leather loafers, at $39.75 per. From Casimir's she bought four pairs of Italian low-heeled shoes with gold buckles.

Jackie has a thing about shoes. Checking through available records of Jackie's 1969 footware purchases, I have already reached the total of sixty-two pairs, fifteen bought in Rome. It seems safe to say that Mrs. Onassis has in her closets, here and abroad, enough shoes so that she can wear a different pair every day of the year without ever wearing the same pair twice.

At Sona the Golden One, a fancy boutique, Jackie picked up a "churidan," an Indian-style, three piece costume, pants, tunic, and scarf. At Annacat's she collected five ruffled blouses, three in sheer silk, one embroidered voile, and one in cotton lace. Bonnie Cashin, one of America's foremost sportswear designers, told me that Mrs. Onassis had purchased three of her leather coats, at $550 each, at Saks Fifth Avenue.

But the above are bagatelles compared with Jackie's new $40,000 to $60,000 sable coat. And, talking about furs, Mrs. Onassis sailed into Maximilian's one day to get an Alaskan marten fur coat. Also, Mrs. Onassis bought during her big spending spree enough handbags, stockings, lingerie, gloves, and compacts, to name but a few items, to start a boutique of her own.

When Mrs. Onassis, always unannounced, walks into a store, the help, as can be expected, give her more attention than they would give anyone else except a holdup man. "I was in Bonwit Teller's S'fari Room," recalls a visiting Canadian, "when Mrs. Onassis arrived. The salesgirl who had been waiting on me dropped what she was showing me and rushed over to assist Jackie. The manager, assistant manager, other employees, and curious customers clustered around her until it looked like a political rally. I was completely ignored for twenty minutes, until Jackie bought some harem pants and left. I missed my train!"

Not only are customers upset when Mrs. Onassis materializes; the sales help often get so rattled that they are simply useless for the rest of the day. If Jackie is really buying madly, the store, when she leaves, looks like a battlefield after a firefight with the Viet Cong. Open boxes, tissue paper, and order blanks are strewn over the counters. Some exhausted employees slump in their chairs. Others, yet ambulatory, jostle each other to use the phone and call their husbands or boyfriends. And the proprietor and manager, more likely than not, go down the block to celebrate with a snifter.

This is not surprising. When the word gets around that a New York merchant has sold to Mrs. Onassis it is comparable to the honor conferred on a London merchant when he is permitted to have lettered on his window, "By appointment to the Queen."

For example, one Saturday in March, 1969, Mrs. Onassis entered Saint Laurent Rive Gauche on upper Madison Avenue and, as *Women's Wear Daily* later reported, "bought the place out." A lady employed at that establishment told me: "We were all so excited we forgot to make out proper sales slips, and we could not remember some of the things Mrs. Onassis bought. All told, I'm sure she spent $3,000 in maybe ten minutes. One salesman, an emotional young man even when things are calm, had to be taken home in a taxi and put to bed with a sedative."

Naturally, Mrs. Onassis doesn't carry anything out with her. Her purchases are either picked up by her chauffeur —the Onassis car can always find a place to park, New York cops having a warm regard for the mighty—or are delivered the next day by a boy to her apartment.

Because Mrs. Onassis is so often in orbit, her shopping is not confined to these shores. For years, early in the sixties, Jacqueline Kennedy, along with other supporters of *haute couture*, worshipped at the shrine of Hubert de Givenchy, the aristocratic Frenchman whose "little nothing" look they helped bring to the masses. Now Jackie, and other international socialites, have shifted their primary loyalties in Europe to Valentino, a thirty-six-year-old Roman whose hair runs in all directions and whose studio is so heavily perfumed that ecologists might take alarm. "He is now more expensive than ever—$2,500 a gown and way up," said Beverly Pepper, an American artist and sculptor who lives in Rome and moves with the smart fashion and social set. Mrs. Pepper—whose husband, Bill Pepper, is a veteran journalist and best-selling author —told me: "Jackie has bought heavily from Valentino's new fall collection. Valentino always goes to see Mrs. Onassis when he and she are in New York and, being she's Jackie, I wouldn't be surprised if he pops into Skorpios, from time to time."

From another source in Rome I learned that last year Mrs. Onassis enriched Valentino to the tune of more

than $30,000. That is quite a sum, when one realizes that
she deals with many, many designers, and that her entire
clothes bill in the White House for one whole year—a bill
that made the President erupt like Vesuvius—was reported
to be $30,000.

Despite her current crush on Valentino, Jackie is not
neglecting Paris. A spokesman for the designer Cardin
said that she bought "seven or eight" outfits at one time.
Since the average going price at Cardin's is $1,200, that
makes Jackie's last visit there a transaction of somewhere
around $9,000. Nine thousand would go a long way at
Macy's or Marshall Field's. Incidentally, a visit to Cardin's
is old home week for Jackie. The *directrice* is Nicole
Alphand, a tea-party chum from Washington days, when
Nicole's husband was De Gaulle's Ambassador to the
United States.

In Paris, Jackie ordered from Grès a *djelabba* that she
first saw pictured in *Vogue*. Other leading houses, like
Saint Laurent and Courrèges, also say Jackie was a good
client last year. They all keep on hand her dummy,
an exact reproduction of her silhouette, so that she can
order by cable, phone, or mail, just as you or I would
from a Sears-Roebuck catalog.

Jackie's astronomical clothes budget boggles the average working girl, but those in the golden social world
expect it of her. From her vantage point, fashion colum-
ist Eugenia Sheppard isn't suprised by a $300,000 outlay,
which is a knowledgeable estimate of Jackie's current
annual clothes bill. Miss Sheppard says that $20,000
annually is the absolute minimum for which a fastidious
woman of fashion can cover her nakedness, while a really
clothes-conscious aspirant for international consideration
will spend upward of $100,000 a year on dresses alone.

And Mrs. Onassis is no ordinary "clothes-conscious aspirant." She is a walking bank.

Wherever she shops—New York, London, Rome, Paris,
Athens, or, for that matter, Reykjavik, Iceland—she never
pays for anything in cash or produces a check or credit
card. Jackie's face is her charge plate.

While Jackie might appear to be buying willy-nilly, she
is not. She does buy often, but she always buys well. A
couple of years ago Marilyn Bender, the New York
Times's fashion reporter, wrote: "Jacqueline Kennedy has
the lean, flat-chested figure of a model and the taste
and convictions of a fashion editor, which she might have
been."

Being a talented sketch artist, Jackie, since she was a
little girl, has been drawing the kinds of clothes she
would like to have. In 1951 her friends and family insisted
that she enter the *Prix de Paris*, the annual contest held by
Vogue. The prize, a superb reward, was a job for six
months in *Vogue*'s Paris office.

Jackie won. Her school chums flipped. Her mother was
delighted. But Jackie yawned. Hr-hum, she'd been to
Paris often—and had spent one year at the Sorbonne. She
had other worlds to conquer.

While the fashion magazine business missed Jackie's
editorial talents, her sister Lee upheld the Bouvier honor
in that field. Lee became an assistant to fashion's Empress
in Residence, Diana Vreeland, when Mrs. Vreeland was
fashion editor of *Harper's Bazaar*, and Lee has modeled
for *Vogue* since Mrs. Vreeland became its editor-in-chief.

Mrs. Vreeland often tried to induce Jackie to pose for
Vogue cameramen, but each time her request was re-
jected. Actually, Jackie is a friend of Mrs. Vreeland's, and
she admires the editor for her dictatorial tastes. When

Jackie makes up her mind that a style is good, nothing, not even a Presidential veto, can change it. And when Mrs. Vreeland assembles the staff to decide on what styles will be featured in the next issue (she already has made *her* choice), she begins the meeting by saying: "If anyone has anything stupid to say, will they please step outside."

Jackie's desire to be always turned out in sensational clothes was partly sparked, in her youth, by an intense if undeclared fashion war with Lee. Although Lee is three and a half years younger, many people who know both women say she always had a keener instinct for the right things to wear, for "pushy eye-catchers." An early example of Bouvier *vs.* Bouvier was given one night, when Jackie was seventeen, at a Newport party in the famous Clambake Club. After days of contemplation, Jackie decided to "play it straight" that night, and she wore a demure, proper, puff-sleeved and bouffant white gown, just as every young deb should. Suddenly every eye turned toward the door in amazement. It was fourteen-year-old Lee, making a grand entrance, in a strapless, shimmering gown she had smuggled into her home past her sister and her mother. Lee stole the show hands down.

Jackie, who hadn't even known her sister would be at the party, was fit to be tied. But she made up for that night the following year when society columnist Cholly Knickerbocker named her "Debutante of the Year." He said Jackie was regal enough to be a real queen and possessed the grace of "Dresden porcelain."

All their lives, the two sisters have been trying to outdo each other in the clothes department. Lee, by her own admission, has fallen behind since Jackie married a President, then the Greek tycoon with the bottomless purse.

"At this stage of the game," one of their mutual friends told me, "the only chance Lee has of outshining Jackie is if the international jet set wholeheartedly adopts nudity."

These days, Jackie's importance to the women's wear industry is such that if she should suddenly lose interest in being smartly turned out, and go around wearing anything that was handy, like a latter-day Hetty Green, there would be deep despair and the gnashing of teeth on Seventh Avenue.

When John Kennedy was inaugurated in 1961, the fashion industry had, in the new First Lady, a super-consuming goddess. Speaking for the trade, John Fairchild bowed his editorial head, bent his knee, kissed the hem of her garment, and dubbed Jackie "Her Elegance." Everything Jackie wore set a new style. And why not? The Gallup Poll's professional snoopers had just found her to be "The most adored woman in the world." The *Ladies Home Journal* said: "Jackie's slightest fashion whim triggers seismic tremors up and down Seventh Avenue."

When Jackie raised her skirts—almost to mini-length—shortly after entering the White House, the sound of scissors shortening dresses on Seventh Avenue was almost deafening. When Jackie wore a mantilla, it was the proudest moment for Spain since Cortez conquered Mexico. After Jackie was photographed with her arms and legs bare, except for those long white gloves, the stocking people went into panic. And Jackie's Somali leopard coat—an instant sensation—caused more fatalities among the leopard population than anything since the great jungle plague of 1309.

Jackie also did wonders for low shoes, fur skiing hoods, berets, English riding clothes, one-piece maternity dresses (when she was expecting John), and she's become the patron saint of the people who manufacture sunglasses. Jackie's black boots and pillbox hat were blessings to the booteries and practically rescued the milliners from economic oblivion.

Students of the Kennedy Era should be aware that the placing of the pillbox hat on Jackie's head was preceded by the type of political maneuvering more often associated with the passing of a bill to benefit alfalfa growers. When John Kennedy was making his bid for the Democratic nomination in 1960, the millinery industry was dumbstruck when it discovered that Mrs. Kennedy didn't have so much as a single bonnet to her name. They faced ruin if America had a hatless First Lady. Lobbyists charged into action, armed with votes, contributions, and hospitality hotel suites stocked with bourbon. Kennedy backers were told, quite bluntly, that unless Mrs. Kennedy covered her head, her husband had as much chance of getting the milliners' votes as George Wallace had of being endorsed by the Harlem Globetrotters.

Smart politicians never argue on such matters. John Kennedy got the message to his wife, and one day, at Jackie's request, Bergdorf Goodman sent to her suite in the Waldorf Towers—where she was staying on a visit to New York—a salesman with an assortment of samples. Jackie chose the pillbox, by Dior, and pictures of her, wearing it, appeared in newspapers all over the country.

(Around the time Jackie was wearing boots and the pillbox hat, which had a military cut to it, historian Barbara Tuchman, the author of *The Guns of August*, said: "American fashion is being taken over by the pansy boys. We're being made to look like Lolitas and lion tamers. All those boots and helmets!")

Fashion-minded people go to great lengths to find out

what Jackie is wearing and who made it, and this can be a
nuisance to her. When she goes to a public place, she is
reluctant to part with her wrap or coat. She fears the hat
check girl will look at the label and spill the beans and
the press wire services will send bulletins around the
earth. Designers or milliners or furriers who leak to the
press details of Jackie's purchases will never again, if
they are found out, be beneficiaries of her patronage.
Oleg Cassini, who designed Jackie's inaugural gown and
who, in a two-year period, made three hundred exclusive
models for her consideration, practically evicted a journalist from his office for asking about the First Lady's forthcoming dresses.

"What the hell!" said the newsman. "You'd think I had
asked the Joint Chiefs of Staff about our atomic secrets."

The day Jackie married Aristotle Onassis, newspapers
reserved columns of space for detailed reports on her
trousseau. To the fortunate few present, it appeared that
Jackie was downright radiant in a georgette ivory chiffon
and lace two-piece mini-dress, with long sleeves.

However, since her marriage to the Greek had made her
a controversial goddess, her trousseau became the cause
of a strident debate. In New York she was lauded by
the mods and swingers for breaking tradition, but in
Rome she was castigated for being joined in holy matri-
mony with her knees showing.

In London the American-born dressmaker Robert
Blackwell led the hounds. He placed Jackie high on his
list of the worst-dressed women in the world, crying: "She
did everything to make herself look seventeen, which I
thought was very rude when she was marrying someone
twice her age. She looked more like his daughter than
his wife. If she had any respect for him she would have

worn a tailored dress and looked like a woman, not a child."

Later, the Parisian designer Coco Chanel, an ageless veteran who might almost have run up little peasant garb for Joan of Arc, had pretty much the same thing to say. Miss Chanel, who is the subject of Alan Jay Lerner's hit musical *Coco*, has said of Jackie: "She has horrible taste. She tries to look like her own little daughter by wearing little-girl clothes."

With this candid judgment Miss Chanel violated the ancient and sacred rule of merchandising which says: "The customer is always right." Jackie, through the year, has fattened Coco's till by thousands and thousands. She wore an off-white Chanel suit with black braid edging when she entertained Empress Farah Diba of Iran at the White House in 1962 during the Shah's state visit. And she was wearing a pink-and-navy Chanel suit in Dallas the day John Fitzgerald Kennedy was assassinated.

Actually, since she became Mrs. Onassis, Jackie's clothes seem less showy, more homey. In New York's Le Pavillon, center of the high fashion swirl, luncheon patrons chatter about Jackie's new look—and there's a babel of opinions. Still, there seems to be general agreement that today's wardrobe is more "real"; after all, with one billion dollars to lean on, Jackie doesn't have to impress anybody but herself. Bonnie Cashin put Jackie under her clinical X-ray and said: "Mrs. Onassis dresses almost conservatively, she is not at all *avant garde*. She is not at all an innovator and her wardrobe is strictly status quo." Bonnie has plenty of supporters. Eleanor Lambert, one of our leading fashion publicists, told me: "Jackie now dresses like a very happy woman. Not so stiff, even careless, once in a while."

Now, let's see where in Manhattan Jackie whiles away her days in shopping, dining, and just playing.

HOW TO SHOP IN MANHATTAN
ON ONLY $50,000 A DAY

Chief Purveyors to Her Majesty in
Jackie O.'s Wonderful World of New York

COUTURIERS

Chez Ninon   487 Park Avenue
No bargain basement this; the price range for a custom-made evening gown—$2,000 to $4,000.

House of Cassini   445 Park Avenue
The former First Lady's court dressmaker during the Kennedy Administration.
(These days, Mrs. Onassis has most of her dresses made in Rome or Paris.)

BOUTIQUES

St. Laurent Rive Gauche   855 Madison Avenue
Where Paris' aging *enfant terrible* peddles his off-the-rack gew-gaws.

Adolfo's   22 East 56th Street
You can't just breeze into this private custom salon; it's by appointment only. It's also a jewel box—crystal chandeliers and brandy-colored carpets. Hats begin at $55, blouses at $100, pantaloons at $175, and maxi coats at $300.

Veneziano Boutique, Inc.   819 Madison Avenue
Jackie adores Veneziano's pants—particularly those striped like barber poles. Veneziano has pajamas that go for $350. Everything's from Italy, of course.

Sona the Golden One   11 East 55th Street
The source of those exotic caftans and other etceteras is India, of course.

Annacat   924 Madison Avenue
Among other delights, there are those cool low-heeled

Italian shoes with the gold buckles. When the shoes wear out, you've still got the buckles.

Jax, Manhattan, Inc.   *7 West 57th Street*
Jax made its sterling reputation by getting fashionable bottoms into pants. But if you're not lean-shanked—much over size 9—forget it. Jax phones Jackie when anything "hot" arrives.

Halston, Ltd.   *33 East 68th Street*
Barbra Streisand featured Halston hats on one of her TV spectaculars. He's one of the last great milliners in a hatless era. Halston also designs wigs. Well, a wig is a kind of hat, isn't it?

APPAREL SPECIALTY STORES

Bonwit Teller   *Fifth Avenue and 56th Street*
Jackie O. gets her lingerie here and often forages around the S'fari Room.

Henri Bendel   *10 West 57th Street*
On the main floor of this boutique-filled emporium, Jackie shops for such gift items as leatherbound notepads, glorious silver and jade jewelry, oversized polka-dot picnic napkins and multi-colored felt shoulder bags.

Saks Fifth Avenue   *Fifth Avenue and 50th Street*
Jackie O. buys her sweaters here.

Bergdorf Goodman   *Fifth Avenue and 58th Street*
Jackie Kennedy got her inaugural gown here.

Best & Company   *Fifth Avenue and 51st Street*
Everyone who's anyone gets her English perambulator here and outfits her privileged children in the Lilliputian Bazaar.

Lord & Taylor   *Fifth Avenue and 38th Street*
This somber institution is now in the new boutique groove with its Young New Yorker Shop. The YNY Shop is advertised for girls from 19 to 30—which is why it's attracting girls from 30 to 60.

FURRIERS

Jacques Kaplan   730 Fifth Avenue
To give the less fortunate *their* chance, Mr. Kaplan introduced Japanese mink coats with horizontally worked pelts for about $1,000. He's truly charitable. Needless to say, he doesn't waste Mrs. Onassis' time with such trivia.

Ben Kahn Furs Corp.   150 West 30th Street
When Jackie wore Ben Kahn's Somali leopard coat, *every* female on earth squealed with joy—except female leopards.

Harry and Dan Grossman   333 Seventh Avenue
Jackie has one of their "knock-about" sables. Some say it cost $40,000; others say $60,000.

Maximilian Fur Co., Inc.   20 West 57th Street
Creator of Jackie's eye-popping double-breasted mink. Not the sort of thing for trips to the laundromat.
(Each year these furriers exhibit their models in private showings before letting the "general" public see them. At that time the social registrite *and* the non-social big spender can buy a coat or jacket as is—or with her own ideas included.)

JEWELERS

David Webb, Inc.   7 East 57th Street
The public is welcomed into David Webb's pearl-gray emporium—a series of small viewing rooms. There it might see this master jeweler's $63,000 black pearl necklace edged with diamonds and emeralds, or his simpler Etruscan gold jewelry with its rich hammered-looking finish—a wide cuff bracelet embossed with lions is $1,000.

Tiffany & Co.   727 Fifth Avenue
Available is "The Uncut Decision," the name for an 80-carat, uncut diamond. If you have an extra $2,000,000 or so, you can buy it—and *you* may decide how it's to be cut.

Van Cleef & Arpels, Inc.   744 Fifth Avenue
Its private sales salon, for Rolls Royce clients, features—

like a shrine—a richly framed, signed photograph of Jacqueline Bouvier Kennedy Onassis.

Cartier, Inc.   *Fifth Avenue and 52nd Street*
Its Paris and New York branches have been catering to Mr. Onassis for several decades. When Ari feels like buying some gifts he phones Cartier's to send a sack of gems to his home for leisurely inspection. Recently, Mr. O. became co-owner of the Fifth Avenue blockfront that houses Cartier. His investment? $13,000,000.

SHOES

Casimir   *20 East 69th Street*
Strictly imported—and expensive. Jackie also buys footware at the boutiques. She takes a size 10A.

HANDBAGS

Gucci   *Fifth Avenue and 54th Street*
The New York branch of Florence's master leatherworker, Gucci popularized morocco leather handbags with bamboo handles; Jackie adores hers.

Henri Betrix, Inc.   *702 Madison Avenue*
Snakes and other reptiles are *in* right now. Betrix has a 10-by 8-inch handbag in black-dyed crocodile skin for $550, plus sales tax.

Martin van Schaak   *230 East 70th Street*
Mr. van Schaak, you must know, does not have a store—heaven forbid! He's only the most exclusive handbag salesman in New York—and he's *not* interested in the average person. He brings samples of his custom-made wares to client's homes—on invitation only. He incorporates his own smashing designs with his clients' ideas. His evening bags in brocade begin at $175.

LUGGAGE

Mark Cross   *707 Fifth Avenue*
Going traveling? Consider Mark Cross's made-to-order alligator suitcase, a mere $2,200. And they'll show you the proper way to pack it—free!

RIDING APPAREL

Miller's   123 East 24th Street

At any American fox hunt, you'll find Miller's jodhpurs, breeches, and boots. Jackie has been riding to hounds since she was 12—so has Caroline Kennedy.

H. Kauffman & Sons   139 East 24th Street

Miller's neighbor, Kauffman's—est. 1875—has outfitted many generations of the horsey set. Also dude ranchers.

DEPARTMENT STORES

Bloomingdales   Lexington and 59th Street

Gimbels   Broadway and 33rd Street

Ohrbach's   5 West 34th Street

(Jackie doesn't ride department store escalators seeking bargains. She sails in for a specific item, usually one she's seen advertised in the *Times*, or she shops by phone or mail.)

TOYS AND GAMES

F. A. O. Schwartz   745 Fifth Avenue

Mankind's poshiest toy store. A giant teddy bear can cost as much as a real one.

HAIRDRESSER

Kenneth   19 East 54th Street

Kenneth combs the best-known real and fake tresses in America—Mia Farrow's for one.

COSMETICS

Erno Laszlo Institute for Skin Care   677 Fifth Avenue

For years Jackie Onassis has visited Dr. Laszlo—14 times— to have her skin analyzed, and she uses gallons of his made-for-her-alone lotions. Rose Kennedy, Ethel Kennedy, Audrey Hepburn, Anita Colby and the Duchess of Windsor —all worrying about dry skin, oily skin and/or wrinkles— are Dr. Laszlo's personal patients. His prices are high but we all have seen the results. His products for commoners are at Saks Fifth Avenue.

Lanvin-Charles of the Ritz   461 Park Avenue
Among other things, Arpege, My Sin, and Ritual, a "body perfume" in a spray at $6.50 the ounce.

Kenneth   19 East 54th Street
Jackie's hairdresser has been moonlighting in cosmetics, His 1969 sensation was the first breast makeup. A must for topless waitresses or ladies in *Oh! Calcutta!*

ART SHOPS AND GALLERIES

A La Vieille Russie   Fifth Avenue and 60th Street
This has to be one of the finest emporiums of *objets d'art* in the New World. Three thousand dollars for an antique cigarette box is a mere pittance.

Davis Galleries   231 East 60th Street
The number-one American house for superb English watercolors.

Parke-Bernet Galleries   980 Madison Avenue
Where you can spend a pleasant afternoon bidding for a Rembrandt and similar baubles.

DECORATORS

Billy Baldwin   235 East 60th Street
The jet-set's darling, Billy, can make an East Village crash pad look like Versailles—for, oh, $250,000. Ladies like Greta Garbo and Mrs. William Paley won't dare shift as much as as picture without Billy's approval.

Mrs. Henry ("Sister") Parrish   22 East 69th Street
Old Money's darling, "Sister" Parrish gave Jackie some tips on how to jazz up the White House.

RESTAURANTS

La Grenouille   3 East 52nd Street
Here you'll find élite designers (like Bill Blass), decorators, editors, and buyers making snide remarks about one another (over marvy snails) in English, French, Italian and, for all we know, Esperanto.

Prix Fixe—Lunch, $9.55. Dinner, $14.75.

Lafayette   202 East 50th Street
When Jackie and her sister, Lee Radizwill, happen to be in
Gotham simultaneously, they retreat to Lafayette for lunch
and girl talk.

Le Pavillon   111 East 57th Street
The late Ludwig Bemelmans, trencherman *par excellence*,
allowed that this was the best French restaurant in the
entire world! Yes, including Paris. Not everyone would
agree today, but one clique of gourmets still feels it is.
Also, it's the most expensive.

La Côte Basque   5 East 55th Street
If you don't have a recognizable *in* face, you still *might* get
a table here, but it will be in the vicinity of Pittsburgh.
Jackie and Ari are dinnertime devotees.

La Caravelle   33 West 55th Street
It's generally assumed that the late Joseph P. Kennedy
helped bankroll La Caravelle as his personal tribute to
haute cuisine. Practically a club for the Clan Kennedy.

Colony   30 East 61st Street
Oh, so *social*. Particularly at lunch.

21   21 West 52nd Street
The main attraction? *Names.* President Richard Nixon, Ari
Onassis, Ed Sullivan, politicians, theatrical folk and Wall
Streeters at the tables; newspapermen at the bar. Maybe
they can't afford the chow.

Trader Vic's, Plaza Hotel   Fifth Avenue and 59th Street
Appointed liked an escapist's dream of Tahiti, this eatery
serves exotic Polynesian, Japanese and Chinese dishes.

Serendipity 3   225 East 60th Street
For ice cream, plain and fancy, and classic frozen hot
chocolate. Caroline and John Kennedy dig the foot-long hot
dogs with Texas-style chili as well.

NIGHT CLUBS, SUPPER CLUBS, DISCOTHÈQUES AND SALOONS

Hippopotamus   154 East 54th Street
A psychedelic discothèque on the site of the late Arthur, it's frequented by the same beautiful swingers. No Rotarians need apply.

P. J. Clarke's   915 Third Avenue
The last stand of the Irish saloon on revived Third Avenue, P. J.'s includes sawdusted floors, snarling waiters and stoned celebrities.

El Morocco   307 East 54th Street
Still has zebra stripes and a Lester Lanin band playing gentle music to talk by.

La Maisonette, St. Regis Hotel   Fifth Avenue and 55th Street
Middle-aged dancing and singers, like Patachou, Hildegarde and—are you ready for this?—Earl Wilson, Jr.

Chez Vito   36 East 60th Street
Very romantic—if you can tolerate strolling violinists.

Raffles   783 Fifth Avenue
A private club—the admission fee is $2,000—always wall-to-wall with jet-setters.

Cafe Carlyle   35 East 76th Street
Jackie goes to this intimate little cafe to dig Bobby Short, who plays and sings the whole night long.

Elaine's   1703 Second Avenue
This haven for newspapermen, authors and publishers features Elaine—what more can one say.

Mykonos   349 West 46th Street
Greek singers, bouzouki music, folk dancing and some plate smashing.

Athena East   1230 Second Avenue
Another Greek cabaret, one of Ari's old hangouts. Yummy *taramsalata.*

On the fashion pages and in the magazines, there's Jackie in Capri in a flapping black pullover and sandals that clack on the cobblestones along the quay. There's Jackie in Crete wearing a pair of sailor pants; many buttons in front, bell bottoms that flap in a good breeze, the whole thing, very salty. And then there's Jackie cavorting with her children in Central Park, sporting a smart pair of Wrangler jeans. Gone on such occasions is the look of "Her Elegance" that was dignity itself at state dinners (when she condescended to attend them). Gone is the elegance she showed during the classic visit to Paris when her clothes had the metropolis cheering its approval. Jackie's formal attire was such a hit in France that when her husband, the President, rose to speak, before General de Gaulle and other leaders of the Republic, he said, by way of identifying himself: "I am the man who accompanied Jacqueline Kennedy to Paris."

In Paris, Jackie, the clotheshorse, amused President, Kennedy, even thought most of the time her consumption of hard currencies for things to put on her back caused him much grief. Aristotle Onassis is a different story. He is delighted that his wife is having fun and games in the shops and fitting rooms of two continents. "God knows, Jackie has had her years of sorrow," he said recently. "If she enjoys it let her buy to her heart's content."

Who, really, is the man who can afford to say such a pleasing thing? After all, to most of us Aristotle Onassis, playboy and superdealer, is still a cloudy figure—the average citizen knows few of the hard facts about him. Where are his roots? What are his true talents? And how did he make all those millions?

PART THREE

The Legend
of
Aristotle
Onassis

Chapter Nine

HOW TO BE A
BILLIONAIRE

An astonishing fact, in this age of declining feudalism and galloping inflation, is that it is easier to make a million dollars than ever before.

In the United States alone, as a matter of statistical fact, every twenty-four hours at least three more Americans are eligible to join the select Millionaires' Club. In 1969 the number of millionaires in the United States reached 110,000 (according to a projection prepared by the Census Bureau), an increase from 100,000 just eight years before, for an average of 1,250 new millionaires a year.

No one can give the definitive formula for "How to Make a Million," but if anyone has the right to try, it's J. Paul Getty, the oil man. "Almost without exception," says Mr. Getty, "there is only one way to make a great deal of money—and that is in one's own business."

One of those who carefully heeded Mr. Getty's advice about the opportunities in self-employment was Aristotle Onassis, who became an entrepreneur early in his life. Certainly, there was nothing in his background to indicate a bloodline of financial accomplishment.

Ari was born in a broken-down shack in the Greek quarter of Smyrna in Turkey sometime around 1906; no one, not even Ari, is sure of the exact date. His father peddled trinkets on the streets and his mother took in washing, which was a classic beginning for this century's foremost Horatio Alger story, a story that well might be titled: *From Mama at the Washtub to Jackie on the Yacht.* In one of those periodic race-hate riots that for centuries plagued Asia Minor, the Turks commenced massacring the Greek minority who lived among them. During the fury, the family of Aristotle Onassis was decimated. Years later Ari told a journalist: "I saw three of my uncles hanged."

The surviving Onassises fled to Greece, Ari shirtless, clad only in a pair of old pants. In Greece, already a poor nation, the refugees from Turkey were considered a public burden—and a public nuisance. The only education the boy received was in the streets. But Ari did not, like so many other victims, sink into the lethargy of the hopelessly poor. He had big dreams and he knew that, to achieve them, he must escape.

Ari haunted the waterfronts, commencing a love affair with the sea that would last a lifetime. Finally, after months of badgering the captains of the ships in the area, he was taken on as a pantry boy on a rotting Greek freighter, at a wage of twenty-three cents a day.

Fifteen-year-old Ari didn't have a clue as to where the tramp was heading, and he found the meager food and living conditions hardly better than his previous life. Roaches roamed the tramp, and the officers were not above giving the pantry boy a kick in the butt when something irked them. When Ari got his first shore leave, in Buenos Aires, he quietly packed his worldly possessions, which comfortably fitted into one small handbag, and jumped ship. Buenos Aires had a large Greek population that had a warm heart—and ready handouts—for the freshly arrived, curly-haired boy from the old country. They found him a place to stay and helped him get a job with the telephone company, where he was trained as a welder. Ari showed an immense capacity for hard work, a capacity that would help him climb to the heady heights. Shortly after he was employed on the day shift the manager announced time-and-a-half for anyone caring to work overtime. Onassis promptly volunteered.

"How much overtime will you work?" he was asked.

"All night," replied Ari.

Working two shifts, he got along on four or five hours sleep, which is still his habit. (Some people say Onassis works twenty-four hours each day. Not long ago Jackie Onassis made this comment: "Ari *never* stops working. He dreams in millions.")

By living on canned goods and cheap bread, and by ignoring the fleshpots of the city, Onassis saved most of his earnings. Soon he had a comfortable nest egg, and at the age of seventeen he did what Paul Getty advises. He quit his job with the telephone company and became an importer and vendor of cigarettes made of Turkish tobacco, the type favored by the immigrants from Greece and the Levant, who preferred them to Virginia tobacco. Onassis's venture was instantly successful and surprisingly profitable, considering that it was a one-man operation.

It was whispered that Onassis, the Tobacconist, had such a favorable profit margin, because he obtained his merchandise in a highly irregular fashion. It was said that his suppliers were crew members on vessels that called at Greek and Turkish ports and smuggled the cigarettes ashore tax free.

The authorities became suspicious, but they had no concrete evidence to warrant cracking down on young Onassis. Then one evening an oversized Bulgarian sailor, who had several times been seen in Ari's company, was seized by customs men as he walked down the gangplank. He was taken to a police station and forced to strip. It was revealed that he held a pack of cigarettes under each arm, and many more packs were taped to his ankles, calves, thighs, abdomen, and, of all places, his very expansive rump.

The customs inspectors, triumphant, demanded that the seaman admit he had smuggled the cigarettes in behalf of Onassis. But the man, maintaining the tight-lipped loyalty that has ever been a characteristic of Mr. Onassis' confederates, denied this accusation. He could not deny that he had violated the law against importing more than one pack, tax free, but he swore that he had done so, not for gain but as a gift for his local girl friend, a Turko-Greek belly dancer.

Whatever the hard facts of Ari's cigarette venture, by the time he was twenty-four, in 1930, he had amassed $100,000, which in that time and place was worth almost $1,000,000 by today's standards.

During the last four decades, as Aristotle Onassis' empire has grown to incredible proportions, he has had to employ thousands of people, and, accordingly, install rather conventional systems of budget control and personnel hiring methods. Often, discussing his career, he is amused by his elevation into a corporate structure. One time recently, while in New York, he examined the form a prospective employee must fill out if he wants to join an Onassis firm. Ari remarked that "never in a million years would *I* qualify for employment with an Onassis company. In my youth I was a job-hopper and I have always been a maverick and I guess, deep down, I am very nonestablishment, although I favor capitalism and would never join the Students for a Democratic Society."

One of Ari's favorite pastimes is discussing, with old friends like J. Paul Getty, the place of the oddball in today's heavily organized scheme of things, and how, almost without exception, the man who himself makes a million dollars *is* an oddball. Onassis keeps, on his desk on the *Christina*, a copy of Getty's book, *How to Be Rich*, with the following passages heavily underlined:

"The nonconformist, the leader and originator, has an excellent chance to make his future in the business world. He can wear a green toga instead of a gray flannel suit, drink yak's milk rather than martinis, drive a Kibitka instead of a Cadillac, and vote the straight Vegetarian ticket—and it will not make the slightest difference. Ability and achievement are *bona fides* no one dares question, no matter how unconventional the man."

Mr. Onassis also has clippings from the London *Sunday Times* on an exhaustive study that worthy publication made, in the United States and the United Kingdom, of today's millionaires. Among other things the *Times* learned about Onassis, and others of equal accomplishment, was that "Mr. Millions is a gambler on a colossal scale. He forms his judgment after the most exhaustive examination, but having done so he proceeds to back his judgment to the whole extent of his personal fortune."

That's exactly what Mr. Onassis did right after he had accumulated his first pile in cigarettes—he gambled everything. And the year he dared to risk what he had made, at such effort, was 1930, in the time of the Great Depression, the year of "Brother, Can You Spare a Dime?" Mr. Onassis had had it with the cigarette business, and had long been eager to get into shipping.

Twenty years later, Onassis recalled: "Ships all around the world were laid up because of the Depression. You could pick up a ship for the same price as a Rolls Royce."

He bought six freighters from the Canadian National Railways at $20,000 apiece—they had been built ten years before at a cost of $2,000,000 each. He went for broke, maintaining the vessels in seaworthy condition during the dark days. Several years later, when business improved and the nations started arming themselves for the forthcoming Second World War, his ships were booked solid, and his fortune multiplied with astronomical rapidity.

Most European shippers lost the better part of their fleets to U-boats during the war. Onassis was more fortunate. By luck, or by design, most of his vessels were in neutral countries, like Sweden, when hostilities broke out. So, when the war ended, Onassis, with his fleet intact, was in the driver's seat. The world was in desperate need of civilian ships, any kind of ships. Naturally, Onassis could, and did, demand outrageous prices to haul cargoes.

More than once, through the years, Mr. Onassis has been at odds with the United States government. The first time was in the early 1950's, shortly after the State of Israel, with American moral and financial support, was formed. The Arabs, stunned by their defeat at the hands of the Israelis, began to boycott every product made by foreign concerns that also did business with Israel. For example, Coca-Cola, long a favorite with the non-alcoholic Arabs, was eventually banned because the parent company had franchised a bottling plant in Israel. (Illegal Cokes went for a dollar a bottle in Baghdad.)

Onassis was kept informed of the growing Arab boycott by his many agents in the Middle East. Logically, it is an area that interests him greatly; his primary business is carrying oil, and oil does not come from Finland. In any case, Onassis heard that a powerful anti-U.S. block inside Saudi Arabia, headed by Jamal Hussein, a cousin of the Grand Mufti of Jerusalem, wanted Saudi ships to carry Saudi oil, instead of relying on foreign vessels, primarily vessels owned by the Arabian-American Oil Company (Aramco) and flying the American flag.

In a scene out of Arabian nights, Onassis was brought into contact with Hussein and a contingent of bearded sheiks. Appealing to their nationalism, he proposed to build and operate a Saudi tanker fleet, flying the Saudi flag. In return for this service, Onassis would reserve for himself the right to carry ten percent of Saudi oil in his own tankers, a concession that would probably have netted him as much money as any other man on this earth. The London *Telegraph*, commenting with awe on this bold scheme, said: "Indeed, Aristotle Onassis has colossal gall, but it must also be said he has the imagination and, apparently, the resources that are given to the leaders of few independent nations."

The Onassis proposal was discussed, in the traditional manner of Arabia, at endless parleys and endless feasts. One night Onassis, whose stomach was disturbed after yet another banquet of roasted lamb, remarked to an associate: "If Alka-Seltzer is in the red this year, they can't blame me."

As the negotiations dragged on, the shipbuilders of Western Germany, who expected that if Mr. Onassis made a favorable arrangement with the Saudi Arabians *they* would get fat construction orders, suggested that Ari retain the services, as an advisor, of Dr. Hjalmar Schacht, who had been the financial wizard of Nazi Germany. (Herr Schacht was the only man who could make Adolf Hitler understand that even his Thousand-Year Reich had to have financial savvy; Britain's wartime Foreign Secretary, Anthony Eden, once said that Schacht was worth ten divisions to the Nazis.) Herr Schacht and Mr. Onassis had cordial meetings in Paris; they had immense respect for each other's appreciation of the realities of power politics. Then Schacht made several cloak-and-dagger trips to the Middle East. In time, when he felt he had grasped all the problems, he used his persuasive salesmanship to convince King Ibn Saud that Saudi Arabia would prosper if it made a deal with the Greek.

When Onassis returned to Arabia to sign the contract, he was received like a long-lost disciple of the Prophet himself. The King gave him a bejeweled dagger—and, for the duration of his stay, placed at his disposal a small harem of "comfort women." (There is nothing in published reports to indicate whether or not Mr. Onassis made more than ceremonial use of either the dagger or the harem.)

When the news of the deal broke in Washington, the State Department was furious. The Soviet Union had begun to infiltrate all of Arabia; Communist arms were going to Syria and Egypt; it appeared that Moscow intended to place a red star over the pyramids. The State Department was fearful that, in the continuing struggle between Israel and the Arabs, the Saudi tankers Onassis was now to build would fall into Russian hands, altering considerably the balance of power. Futhermore, Aramco, with its powerful lobby in Congress, feared a severe setback for American international oil interests. Strange forces—including, without doubt, the CIA—went into action to nullify the Saudi arrangement with Onassis. The U.S. government put the arm on the Saudis. And suddenly Onassis was accused of bringing off his coup by paying some $830,000 in bribes to the Foreign Minister, Sheik Al Suleiman, and to the Minister of Trade, Abdullah Ali Reza.

King Ibn Saud sacked Al Suleiman straightaway, and tore up the contract with Mr. Onassis, and that was that. Except for one thing—several junior functionaries, who had dealt with Onassis or his agents, were taken out and shot. Business in Saudi Arabia can be rough.

Onassis flew back to London to lick his wounds. He told a journalist who dropped into Claridge's to console him: "It isn't every day that a man loses one billion dollars. But what can I do? Declare war on the United States?"

Not long after that, Onassis had another very expensive eyeball-to-eyeball confrontation with the U.S. government. Picture the scene . . .

Friday, February 5, 1954. The Colony, one of New York's fanciest restaurants, is, as usual, crowded this lunch time. At one choice table is a movie star; at another, a dowager sparkling with diamonds like Cartier's window; at a third is Aristotle Onassis, wearing his usual dark shades, a monogrammed cream-colored shirt, and a

pin-striped, double-breasted dark suit made—where else?
—on London's Savile Row. He is deep in conversation with
two other men who also operate on an international scale
and look it.

Onassis, who fourteen years later will marry the widow
of a President of the United States, is toying with his
second dry martini when a somber, bulky man walks
across the elegant room, stops before the table, and asks:

"Mr. Onassis?"

"Yes."

"I'm a Federal Marshal. You are under arrest."

The Marshal took Onassis to Washington, where he was
fingerprinted, mugged, and formally committed to jail,
then promptly released on $10,000 bail.

Onassis had been indicted for "conspiring to defraud the
United States Government" by illegally purchasing several
surplus wartime Liberty ships at bargain-counter prices.
The law specifically forbids non-Americans to acquire
these ships. However, Onassis and other Greek shipowners got them through American "partners" or "fronts,"
including some Very Important People, such as onetime
Secretary of State Edward Stettinius and Congressman
Joseph Casey of Massachusetts. It was a first-rate scandal.

After complicated and extended legal moves and
countermoves, the criminal charges against Mr. Onassis
were dropped when he agreed to pay a $7,000,000 fine.
When asked how he and the United States had arrived
at such a sum, Mr. Onassis said: "Oh, it's easier to deal
in round figures." (The man who represented the government in its suit against Mr. Onassis was the then Assistant
Attorney General Warren Burger, now Chief Justice of
the United States.)

Although Onassis had long been known in the various

financial centers, the first time he splashed into international prominence was in 1952, when he bought a controlling interest in the Société des Bains de Mer, which runs the Monte Carlo Casino.

Long before jets, or prop planes, or, for that matter, the Wright Brothers, Monte Carlo had a kind of jet-set glamour. It was a place where people allegedly traveled from bed to bed with hardly a care, and where fortunes were made and lost on the bounce of a roulette ball, and where the heavy losers, according to hoary tradition, were supposed to kindly go out on the lawn and blow their brains out.

Its reputation was such that even decades ago it worried good Queen Victoria, that stern monitor of a century's morals. One summer day the Queen, according to a substantiated legend, was traveling down the coast of France for a proper holiday in Italy. When the train approached Monte Carlo, she ordered the shades drawn on her private car. She had no intention of looking out on such a wicked place.

When Mr. Onassis was asked if he had bought the Monte Carlo Casino as an investment, he pooh-poohed the idea. Really, he insisted, he had bought the place because it had a lot of empty office space and he had not been able to find enough elsewhere in a decent part of Europe. Also, Monte Carlo's protected bay was an excellent place for a fellow to anchor his yacht, alongside those belonging to such diverse and solvent personages as the American moviemaker Zanuck, the British merchant prince Marks, the German munitioneer Krupp, and the Aga Khan.

With the Casino tucked under his wing, Ari set out to make himself uncrowned King of the Jet Set with the same concentration he had previously devoted to the accumulation of money. He used the Casino and his regal yacht as bait to attract the Beautiful People, and soon Monte Carlo, which had gone into a decline when World War I ended and income taxes, began, was again very much *in*. An integral part of Mr. Onassis' court was made up of unemployed kings, like Umberto of Italy, Michael of Rumania, Peter of Yugoslavia, and the Count of Paris, Henri Louis-Philippe d'Orléans, Pretender to the throne of France. Ari was only too glad, when one of his royal friends was in straitened circumstances, to extend a loan, and it was reported that for a long time Peter of Yugoslavia depended on the Greek to make it unnecessary for him to seek gainful employment.

The social circle that rotated around Ari often created tempting opportunities for deposed, impoverished monarchs. Simeon of Bulgaria, who is six feet two and immensely good-looking, is a fine example. He solved his monetary problems, a few years ago, in the classic manner. He worked very hard on the Riviera. Playing smashing golf. Dancing dreamily at Ari's parties. Looking terrific on a tennis court. And by marrying a multimillionaire Spanish industrialist's five-foot-two daughter.

Ari has always treated the throned and dethroned with deference. When someone asked him whether he was a "friend" of the Prince of Monaco, he answered shrewdly: "I know the Prince. But you do not become the friend of a King by saying you are his friend. *He* has to say you are his friend."

This was something Prince Rainier was very unlikely ever to say. Ari's jet-set activities, and his acceptance by the popular press as the *real* ruler of the tiny principality, rubbed Prince Rainier's sensitive feelings the wrong way, and absolutely infuriated his Princess, the former Grace Kelly of Philadelphia and Hollywood. A few years after Onassis moved into Monte Carlo he was no longer on the palace's list of favorite guests. The Prince wanted to develop his realm in such a way as to make it attractive to middle-class tourists. Ari, never much of a mingler with the masses, liked it fine the way it was. They clashed. Finally, using all the pressure at his command, plus a considerable portion of the public treasury, the Prince forced Ari to sell his shares in the Société des Bains de Mer.

It is not known if Ari's ego was injured by that transaction, which, for all practical purposes, declared him *persona non grata* in Monte Carlo. But it is known that his purse was not injured. For his shares in the Société he received what he had paid for them—plus a $5,000,000 profit.

Although Mr. Onassis has had his problems with the United States and Monaco, he has never, being a man of peace, found himself in a virtual state of war with either. But such was not the case with Peru, which sent its navy against the Greek's seaborne units sixteen years ago.

Early in the 1950's Onassis, who is fascinated by everything that floats, became interested in the whaling industry. With his usual thoroughness, he traveled thousands of miles to visit whaling centers. He spent weeks living aboard the less than fragrant whalers in the icy and turbulent waters off South America, not far from the tip of Antarctica. Finally, his hunch that there was an honest dollar to be made in whaling, supported by his on-the-spot investigation, led him to start buying whaling ships in various parts of the world through undercover agents.

Explaining his preference for staying in the shadows

during such negotiations, he said: "If an item is worth $1,000, it doubles in price the moment the owner hears that Aristotle Onassis is interested in buying it."

Within a few months Onassis was the proprietor of twenty whaling ships, a considerable armada. Choosing, as always, to regard commercial restrictions as so many irritants to the free enterprise system, he encouraged his captains to overlook the offshore fishing rights claimed by most sovereign nations. In August, 1954, twelve ships of the Onassis whaling fleet, flying Panamanian flags and crewed by German sailors, appeared in water regarded, officially, as belonging to Peru. Peru was infuriated by the "invasion." University students demonstrated in the streets. The Lima newspaper *Nación* took a hard line: "The whaling pirate Onassis insists on disregarding our national sovereignty. . . . If he persists he must be brought to book and his ships must be seized."

Ari's response to that threat was given to a United Press reporter, who sent this flash: "Onassis whalers to defy Peru."

If Ari thought the Peruvians were bluffing, he was mistaken. Several Peruvian destroyers steamed toward the Onassis fleet, and units of the Peruvian Air Force circled ominously overhead. Upon being advised that Peru was going to use muscle, Mr. Onassis backed down somewhat and radioed his ships to "use discretion." Some years later he explained: "The only things my boys had to defend themselves with were harpoon guns, and while I am sure they could have given a good account of themselves, they were, after all, employed to catch whales, not as combat troops."

The fleet started to disperse and sail out of the area, but the Peruvian destroyer *Aguirre* cut across the bow of

Onassis' flagship, the massive *Olympic Challenger*, and, simultaneously, five or six bombs splashed in the waters nearby. The destroyer then signaled the *Challenger* to heave to and surrender. The *Challenger* used "discretion." A boarding party of very tough-looking Peruvian marines took command of the flagship and directed her to the nearest port. Before the engagement, which might be recorded in naval history as "The Battle of Onassis," was over, four other whalers were boarded and sailed to port like prizes of war.

Mr. Onassis seemed amazingly placid about his defeat on the high seas and the seizure of his property, valued at $10,000,000. *He* was not concerned about his pocketbook, but the good, gray men of Lloyd's of London, who had insured the whalers for every hour lost, were concerned about theirs. This matter was costing Lloyd's at the rate of £30,000 a day.

The British government, no doubt encouraged by Lloyd's, huffed and puffed about Peru's highhanded methods. Peru was unimpressed. Three weeks later a Peruvian court considered the charge that Mr. Onassis' ships had violated the country's fishing waters, found him guilty, and fined him $3,000,000. (God, does Aristotle Onassis collect fines!) The court said that if Mr. Onassis did not pay up in *five days*, Peru would assume ownership of his ships. What could the man do? Peru might have overreacted, but possession is still eleven points in the law.

Five days later, just under the wire, Mr. Onassis' representative, Roberto Arias, the Panamanian politician who is married to Margot Fonteyn, arrived in Lima with his boss's certified check for fifty million Peruvian sols. Lloyd's had to reimburse Mr. Onassis for this amount, so his own loss was zero. A sol saved is a sol earned.

Two years after the Battle of Onassis, Ari, with his usual foresight, divined that the business of whaling would be, in the immediate future, in sharp depression. Quietly, he unloaded his twenty vessels on Japanese interests. Mr. Onassis earned himself a smart little profit of $8,500,000 on the sale. Not bad. Not bad at all.

Aristotle Onassis is, without question, a financial genius, and maybe more than that. Anyone who has known him, even in passing, has been overwhelmed by his intelligence, his photographic memory, his hypnotic charm, and his ability to analyze, almost at a glance, *your* problems, ambitions, character—and whether or not you are a damn fool.

"Aristotle Onassis doesn't merely speak to you," said an American businessman after spending some time in Ari's office aboard the *Christina*, "he undresses you, X-rays the contents of your wallet, and, by a sixth sense, I am sure, can tell how much money you've got in the bank and if you're a Republican, a Democrat, or a member of the Prohibitionist Party."

You can ask Onassis: "Sir, how much is 875½ times 732¼?" and in a minute, without a pad or pencil, he will give you the correct answer. The *maître d'* at the Hotel de Paris in Monte Carlo, which Onassis once owned, told me: "Onassis can converse fluently in seven languages, but but he thinks in money."

Ari, who is in truth a dropout from kindergarten, is at home in English, French, Italian, Spanish, German, Turkish, and Greek—and he has better than a restaurant smattering of half a dozen other languages.

When I was in Beirut, a few years ago, on a journalistic assignment, I became acquainted with an executive of Pipeline, a subsidiary of Aramco, which had had considerable dealings with Mr. Onassis. "During several relatively brief trips to Cairo, Beirut, Damascus, Baghdad, and the population centers of Saudi Arabia," said the man from Pipeline, "Mr. Onassis—without ever cracking a book or taking a lesson—acquired sufficient Arabic to conduct a limited conversation. Certainly he spoke as much Arabic as most of the Europeans and Americans who have been posted for as long as a decade in North Africa or the Middle East. In fact, I remember that one evening Mr. Onassis attended a reception at the home of the British Ambassador to Lebanon, and during the course of the gathering he conversed with an Arab diplomat. Well, the Ambassador, an old hand in Arabia and the Levant, overheard this and, in admiration, offered Mr. Onassis, in case he was seeking employment, a position as an interpreter."

Concerning Mr. Onassis' ability to learn *anything* with dispatch, Johnny Meyer, the shipowner's primary agent in the United States, once said: "Ari hasn't got a brain, in the conventional sense, he has a blotter, camera, and tape recorder in his head."

You can take a short stroll down a strange street with Mr. Onassis, and when you get to the next block you probably couldn't remember, if you were asked, anything you saw in the block before. But if you asked Onassis, he could tell you exactly what kind of shops lined the street —that one was a butcher shop, the other a grocery, the third sold ladies' apparel, and the fourth was a café, and on and on. Furthermore, he could also recall the pedestrians who passed—that there X number of blue-collar workers, X number of housewives, X number of aged men, probably pensioners, and X number of hustlers; Ari doesn't miss a thing.

A good-humored banker once told me in New York:

"When Onassis dies he should not leave his brain to science. He should leave it to the Manufacturers Hanover Trust. I'm a stockholder."

Onassis has a knowledge of geopolitics—geography plus politics—that has enabled him, time and again, to profit from global crises. When I went to Cairo immediately after the Arab-Israeli Six-Day War, in the summer of 1967, I was told that Onassis had predicted, almost to the day, when the shooting would commence. He also guessed, correctly, that President Gamal Abdel Nasser would once again—as he had during the 1956 desert war—commit all his armor to the Sinai, and that all of it would soon be in ruins. Onassis further assumed that, in a desperate "scorched sands" policy, the Egyptians would block the Suez Canal by scuttling, in that thin waterway, several ships.

The latter—correct—assumption motivated him, many weeks before the first Israeli bomb fell on Egyptian soil, to redeploy his tankers, moving out of the Mediterranean and into the Red Sea. Having done that, he was in an enviable position to haul oil to Europe the long way around. And because freight cargo rates rocketed quickly from $5 to $15 a ton, Onassis is said to have made, since the Six-Day War, at least another $10,000,000.

A man who conducts his business as fiercely as Onassis does must expect to make a lot of enemies, but he denies that he has. "I have no friends or enemies," he said, "only competitors."

But his own comfortable view of those he has bested is not shared by men intimately familiar with his guerrilla engagements in the back alleys of unorthodox finance. The German-American journalist Joachim Joesten, who had written a book about Onassis, said: "Onassis has more enemies than any other public figure one can think of since Hitler and Stalin."

Mr. Joesten was referring to Onassis' cutthroat methods, and whatever Ari's methods really are, he has certainly enraged conservative shipping men. He has been blacklisted by the Norwegian Shipowners' Association and the British Chamber of Shipping, one of whose members said, in an Old School Tie put-down: "That Onassis chap, he reminds me of a hairy spider." One of Onassis' rivals, Stavros Niarchos, who does not claim to be objective, said: "Onassis commits political crimes and economic monstrosities."

Public scandals and name-calling have always trailed Onassis. He is well versed in the court procedures of several countries because he is forever the target of indignant plaintiffs who claim he swiped everything from them but their birthmarks. Some of the best legal talents money can buy in Europe and America, including former U.S. Attorney General Herbert Brownell, have, at one time or another, acted in his defense.

A well-known shipowner who, although he's crossed swords with Onassis—and come away bleeding at the pocketbook—still respects his competitor, said: "Every morning, when Aristotle Onassis gets out of bed, he shaves his face, brushes his teeth, and calls up his lawyer."

So one must regard Mr. Onassis' statement that he has no enemies with skepticism. If he has no enemies, why—for fifteen years now—has he been accompanied everywhere he goes by one or more well-groomed, well-tailored, and very powerfully built gentlemen with bulges in their jackets under the left shoulder? A man without enemies doesn't need bodyguards.

From a long-time Onassis employee, and from a member of the crew of the *Christina,* it was learned that there have been, in recent years, two attempts on his life; neither was reported to authorities. The last occurred three years ago, after Onassis concluded an inspection of one of his tankers docked at Marseilles. A disgruntled sailor, crying that Onassis paid "slave wages," approached him on the pier, flourishing a hunting knife. Onassis' bodyguard quickly subdued and disarmed the belligerent seaman, and briefly used his head for a soccer ball.

The other attempt took place one bright afternoon six years ago when Onassis was taking the sun on the deck of his yacht, anchored off Cannes. A sniper fired three shots which embedded themselves in the bulkhead a few feet away. Mr. Onassis, who has steel nerves, said: "The next time I take the sun I'll protect my skin with a bulletproof vest, not sun tan lotion."

It is extremely doubtful that Onassis could have acquired his staggering wealth if he had operated solely in countries like England or America, where there are enforced taxes and strict laws governing financial manipulations. To Onassis, taxation is an insult, and, if he doesn't like the law in one country, he goes to another. He makes no attempt to camouflage his permanent status as a refugee from the Internal Revenue Services of the world. Speaking with refreshing frankness, he said, a few years ago: "As a Greek I belong to the West. As a shipowner I belong to capitalism. Business objectives dictate the details of my operations. My favorite country is the one that presents maximum immunity from taxes, trade restrictions, and unreasonable regulations."

His favorite countries include such loose-lawed tax sanctuaries as Liberia, Panama, and Honduras, where he has over a hundred corporations that register his ships, now the largest privately owned fleet in the world, to sail under their "flags of convenience."

Tax-free, Mr. Onassis has always managed to preserve a fat percentage of his profits. To show how difficult it would be to do that if one abided by U.S. tax law, let us take the case of Mr. Royal Little. When Little was the $200,000-a-year chairman of Textron, he made this breakdown of what happened to his income:

Wife's household allowance: $24,000
Home improvements: $10,000
Support of mother: $18,000
Charities: $20,000
Taxes: $116,000
Left for myself: $12,000

When Onassis first plunged into the precarious shipping business, he was considered by the Old Guard to be cheeky, and they predicted he would be a flash in the pan. In their arrogance, they gave scant consideration to the possibility that within the skull of the young Greek there resided a unique mind.

While no one any longer questions Ari's business acumen, those who do not know him are inclined to underrate him when they discuss his numerous alliances with glorious women. They put his success on this score down to money alone, and they talk with disdain of his limited height and his harsh peasant features.

They are wrong. The cameras treat Mr. Onassis very poorly, overemphasizing the bags under his eyes and the bulk of his body. In the flesh Ari, while hardly a matinee idol, is of much smoother face and trimmer build. He has gentle eyes and a firm chin and a ready smile. There are few men of his years who carry less fat on their frames, and he has the powerful arms and legs of a wrestler.

Women of all ages and sizes and from all walks of life who meet Onassis sense straightaway his commanding animal magnetism. Miss Gina Lollobrigida, who might be considered an authority in such matters, was recently quoted as saying: "Ari has more sex appeal than any of the pretty faces in Hollywood, or the muscle boys in those weight-lifting magazines."

Indeed, Ari has always made out.

Chapter Ten

THE FIRST MRS. ONASSIS—AND THE OTHER WOMEN IN ARI'S LIFE

Aristotle Onassis treats women in what might be considered an old-fashioned, chivalrous, Knights-of-the-Round-Table manner. He respects them, he defends them, he is their father image and their boy friend at the same time. A gentleman who has known him for several decades told me: "It is hard to compare Aristotle Onassis to any other man in matters of finance *or* the care and handling of females. But let me say this. When money is concerned he is ruthless. When women are concerned he is gallant. These days, when women are demanding equality, and getting more of it than they asked for, he is nothing—now, don't laugh—more nor less than a twentieth-century Sir Walter Raleigh. Sir Walter put his cloak on the ground so a lady could cross a mud puddle without risking a dry-cleaning bill. Onassis puts his yacht in the ocean so a lady can cross the world in security."

This "ruthless with money but gallant with women" remark was seconded, some years ago, by the late Elsa Maxwell, who was long Ari's social counselor. "Women love
Ari," said Miss Maxwell. "Men hate and fear him."

A most frank appraisal of Onassis was offered by a
famous movie star to an associate of mine in Rome. "You
feel instantly," said the actress, "that Ari understands all
your problems and all the problems around you. You are
immediately anxious for him to be your advisor, your pro-
tector. To many of us, when things are coming apart, he is
a sanctuary."

The first woman to become more than a diversion in
Mr. Onassis' life was Tina Livanos, daughter of Stavros
Livanos, another wealthy Greek shipping man. Ari met
Tina during World War II when he visited Mr. Livanos'
suite in New York's Plaza Hotel. Tina was fourteen at the
time, Onassis thirty-seven, but they kind of ignited each
other and Ari hung around playing the role of a lonesome
bachelor "uncle." Their strange relationship, cemented
with double malted milks in Rumpelmayer's Restaurant
(and sweets shop) on Central Park South, continued until
Tina was seventeen, when Ari, with the Old World formal-
ity of a well-rehearsed ballet, asked Livanos *père* for his
daughter's hand. At the same time, he presented Tina
with a gold bracelet inscribed: "T.I.L.Y.," which meant:
"Tina, I Love You." (Square—but effective.)

They were married in 1946 and spent their honeymoon
slowly cruising south down the Inland Waterway to Key
West in a chartered luxury houseboat; then they sailed to
Ari's home in Buenos Aires. Ari had married a child-doll,
one who regarded the kitchen as an unexplored, un-
charted mystery, one who had never boiled an egg and

had no desire to do so, and that is what Ari wanted. He wanted to be the protect-all, the be-all—Daddy O.

Tina and Ari moved easily into the jet set. But their marriage turned out to be an airborne frolic, not the stuff of permanence. She was jealous. There were reports that she hired private detectives to follow him. She suspected him of taking up with every attractive woman in international society.

When the Onassises settled down, if such a phrase can be used for such mobile people, in Monte Carlo, in the Fifties, Ari seemed to be constantly surrounded by beauty. He was forever giving parties honoring such stars of the day as Merle Oberon, Claudette Colbert, Lily Pons, Gene Tierney, and on and on.

Miraculously, Tina and Ari remained married, if in name only, for twelve years. In 1959 Mrs. Onassis appeared in a New York courtroom and claimed that her husband had committed adultery with a "Mrs. J. R.," known to be the separated wife of an American diplomat who spent her time, without her husband, making the party scene on the Riviera.

The big joke, at the time, was that Tina had named only one woman in her proceedings. "She could have named about fifty," said one playboy, "and still have been regarded as extremely considerate of fifty others."

Ari did not contest the suit, and he gladly let her have the divorce, saying: "I do not wish to cross swords with the mother of my children."

When the divorce was granted, Tina said: "It is almost thirteen years since Mr. Onassis and I were married. . . . Since then he has become one of the world's richest men, but his great wealth has not brought me happiness with him, nor, as the world knows, has it brought him happiness with me."

The women in Aristotle Onassis' life were quite dissimilar from one another. It is the nature of this man always to want something different—a different country to travel to, a different companion to travel with. Except when she was jealous, Mr. Onassis' first wife, Tina, was as serene as a lotus pond. Maria Callas perpetually ticked like a time bomb, ready to erupt like Vesuvius. Melina Mercouri was as curious as a cat; every new day and every living thing intrigued her.

But two of the women in Aristotle Onassis' life have amazingly *similar* characteristics—Jacqueline Kennedy and Greta Garbo. Both of them, when they first met Onassis, were already world-famous. Both of them seemed anxious to withdraw from the world. Both of them played (and continue to play) an eternal game of hide-and-seek (or is it peekaboo?) with the press. And both of them seemed to be reborn, to see life afresh, when Aristotle Onassis was at their side.

The story of Onassis' strange (and continuing) friendship with Greta Garbo has been for many years the subject of whispers and rumors and occasional lines of type in the gossip columns. What is the true story?

Although Greta Garbo has not made a movie in almost thirty years, she is still a thrilling figure, even to the long-haired, rock-pop young, who crowd the art museums to see her old productions, and who worship her as if she were the only decent thing on this earth appreciated by their elders.

Onassis first saw Greta Garbo in person during World War II when he moved his headquarters to New York and leased an apartment on the eighteenth floor of the Ritz

Tower Hotel on East 57th Street. By sheerest coincidence, his next-door neighbor was Greta Garbo. Onassis insists (although many doubt him) that he never had any kind of acquaintance with Miss Garbo at the time, except for those stiff nods and gruff "Good mornings" that New York residents reserve for their neighbors when they encounter them in the elevator.

Onassis says his first extended conversation with Miss Garbo took place at a weekend party at Sutton Place, the British countryside manor that belongs to J. Paul Getty. According to people attending Mr. Getty's party, Miss Garbo, who usually is as communicative as Howard Hughes, suddenly found herself talking away madly to Mr. Onassis, telling him all about her life and times, as if she were a cotton picker confessing her sins at a revival meeting.

Mr. Onassis, it is understood, accomplished this miracle by displaying an intimate knowledge of her career and herself, as if he had been, for a quarter of a century, her press agent and psychiatrist. For the first time that any of those present could recall, Garbo came bursting out of her shell, and after dinner she sang Swedish folk songs and, solo, did several Scandinavian dances; then, calling for a bathing suit, she jumped into the pool and splashed about like a puppy gone daft.

There was the Onassis personality at work; he could hang out his shingle on Park Avenue and make another mint practicing psychiatry. The late artist and writer Ludwig Bemelmans once told the editors of *Town & Country:* "When it comes to women, Ari is a combination of Sigmund Freud, Rasputin, and Rudolph Valentino. He might not be a twenty-five-year-old football hero, but he warms up debutantes *and* dowagers like a flame thrower."

Whatever the true beginning of the Onassis-Garbo friendship, it so happened that in the month after the meeting in the living room of J. Paul Getty's mansion Miss Garbo was the guest of Mr. Onassis at the Château de la Croe, which he then occupied on the French Riviera.

The next year, when he bought controlling interest in the Casino, Miss Garbo arrived, in her usual floppy hat and shapeless dress, and registered at the Hôtel de Paris as "Miss Brown," her favorite alias. She attended several of Mr. Onassis' parties, always staying in the background, and never became part of the action until he took her by the hand and spoke to her, whereupon she lit up like a Christmas tree.

One of the actress's biographers, Norman Zierold, noted in his book that Garbo reacted to Ari like a just-opened bottle of champagne—she simply bubbled. "Garbo was very gay in Onassis' presence," wrote Zierold. "At one Monte Carlo club she sang to the accompaniment of violins. The melody was a Greek song, *Saapair*, whose title translates to mean 'I love you.'"

However, even with Onassis at her side, Miss Garbo, if provoked, was likely to lose her cool with the unexpected severity of a land mine. One evening she accompanied Ari to the Casino's *salon privée* and put a few chips on a number on the roulette wheel. Suddenly a gross American female tourist sidled alongside her, like a tugboat docking, and shrieked: "Oh, I bet you're Greta Garbo! Look— *Harry!—Here's Greta Garbo!*"

Garbo panicked. Abandoning several hundred dollars worth of chips on the table, she left the Casino on the double. Before following Miss Garbo to soothe her, Mr. Onassis picked up her chips.

(One time, shopping at Bloomingdale's in New York,

Garbo reacted differently to a stranger. She was riding the escalator when a woman gazed at her in astonishment. "Are you who I think you are?" she asked. "No," said Garbo.)

Garbo's hair-trigger reactions when she was accosted by strangers or badgered by the press are quirks in her character that even the persuasive Mr. Onassis could not get her to alter. (The same problem he has today with Jackie.)

One day the yacht *Christina*, with Garbo aboard, was anchored off Venice. Ari had, sometime before, promised a group of journalists, most of them British, a tour of the yacht and all her wonders. This particular day, as arranged, a small craft from the *Christina* chugged up one of Venice's main canals to the Royal Danieli Hotel, where the press were quartered as Mr. Onassis' guests. They piled in and headed for the yacht. Onassis was waiting to greet the journalists when suddenly he realized he had committed a colossal gaffe. "For God's sake," he cried to the captain, "if Garbo sees them she will jump overboard."

Ari then spoke to Miss Garbo, who had just arrived on deck after her post-lunch siesta, about the impending crisis and asked her to bear with him just this once. But, as Ari had anticipated, she reacted as if she'd been asked if she'd be kind enough to share her bed, just for one night, with a boa constrictor. She *did* threaten to jump overboard, which would have given the photographers on the fast-approaching launch a Page One picture.

There was only one thing to do. Mr. Onassis waved the launch off—and the reporters' curses, which would have won the admiration of a longshoreman, could be heard loud and clear across the waters as they were ferried back to the hotel.

All Onassis could do was to go later himself to the Royal Danieli, apologizing profusely and buying drinks in the bar until the pressmen were in a more mellow frame of mind.

On another occasion, Mr. Onassis invited, on a ten-day Mediterranean cruise, Miss Garbo and the Italian industrialist Giouanni Agnelli, the British tycoon Loel Guinness and his wife, the French apéritif man, André Dubonnet, and the Maharani of Baroda, who wore a twenty-eight-carat diamond affixed to the right side of her nose.

Every time Garbo was aboard, Ari came up with something unusual; one time it was a "Garbo Film Festival." Garbo hadn't known a thing about it. Each night, after dinner, Ari's guests took their places in the *Christina's* jewel of an intimate projection room, and saw a different Garbo movie, some of them absolutely collector's gems and almost impossible to obtain, which Mr. Onassis' agents, in Europe and the United States, had gathered at great cost.

The Garbo Festival included the silent movie *Flesh and the Devil*, in which she co-starred with John Gilbert; *The Mysterious Lady*, another silent, with Conrad Nagel; *Anna Christie*, Garbo's first talkie, with Charles Bickford and Marie Dressler; *Mata Hari*, with Ramon Navarro, who was brutally murdered by two male prostitutes in his Hollywood home two years ago; *Grand Hotel*, with John Barrymore; and the immortal *Ninotchka*, with Melvyn Douglas.

Garbo was emotionally drained as the sometimes cracked and scratchy record of her career flickered on the screen. She laughed at the dated, jerky movements in *The Mysterious Lady*. She and Ari held hands and sat enthralled at her big love scene with John Gilbert in

Flesh and the Devil. (When *Flesh and the Devil* was first screened, in 1927, the New York *Herald Tribune* reviewer said: "Frankly, never in our screen career have we seen seduction so perfectly done.")

Garbo wept when she saw herself again with John Barrymore in *Grand Hotel.* "John is dead," she whispered. Then she sobbed: "Oh, so many of them are dead. Why am I still alive?"

Whereupon she walked out, in the middle of the picture, and leaned on the rail of the *Christina* and looked out to sea. A few minutes later, Ari joined her and tried to halt the Niagara of tears rolling down her cheeks.

("God, that woman can cry—*no one* can cry like Garbo," said Rouben Mamoulian, who directed her in *Queen Christina* more than thirty-five years ago.)

During all these years (and even today) Miss Garbo leaned on Mr. Onassis for his advice on financial matters. An investment advisor who knows who's got the money and how they got it, told me: "I am *sure* that, because of tips Mr. Onassis has given Miss Garbo, she has made at least $1,000,000 in capital gains by buying and selling real estate and securities."

Miss Garbo is most fortunate in her selection of unpaid advisors; another one is Baron Erich Goldschmidt-Rothschild, a debonair man of the world, twenty years her senior, whom she lunches with when she's in New York, at least once a week, at L'Aiglon.

It certainly was very nice of Ari to help Miss Garbo multiply what she had saved in her Hollywood years, but there are some Onassis critics (and they come in division strength) who say he "used" her.

How?

Well, it is true that Onassis has excited women, young

and old, practically since he was born. And women have often played an important role in furthering his social and business careers, which in the jet set, go together like gin and tonic.

Garbo's role in the Onassis scheme of things is that he presented the usually unreachable star at gatherings where businessmen he was courting were present. Under the impact of her presence—the living legend, even if she said nothing more than "Please pass the salt"—some businessmen, perhaps from places no more glamorous than Frankfurt, Lyons, or Kansas City, might be more likely to close a deal.

One jet setter, who was Onassis' guest at a dinner party during which Mr. Onassis placed Miss Garbo next to a paunchy Dutch businessman, said later: "Garbo, and a goodly flow of wine, completely sent this clod of a Dutchman up to Cloud Nine—man, he was living! After dinner Ari and the Dutchman—just the two of them—adjourned for coffee and cognac to Ari's den, where, I learned later, the Dutchman signed a contract the terms of which did not displease Ari, not at all. I'm sure that after he left the *Christina*, the Dutchman hastened back to his hotel room and called Rotterdam and said: 'Mama! Guess who I had dinner with? *Greta Garbo! Ja ja*, Garbo! . . . What did you say, Mama? . . . Oh, yes, also I signed with Mr. Onassis the contract. I hope it was the wise thing to do.' "

We will let others ponder whether or not Mr. Onassis "used" Garbo as window dressing for his elaborate schemes. If so, she probably would have been only too glad to assist him—it would have been for her a fascinating role.

It really isn't important. What is important is that Ari so often brightened the life of this recluse, this dour

Swede who herself had given so many hours of happiness, through her pictures, to millions of people. Onassis gave Garbo happiness, and he really worked at it, as he does at everything he undertakes. He was constantly conjuring up new tricks to amuse her. One time in Monte Carlo he invited her to dine with him in the fabulous penthouse suite of the Hôtel de Paris (which he then owned), which looks out over the Principality of Monaco. When Garbo entered the apartment, the table was set for three, and the third was the aging but still dynamic Sir Winston Churchill.

Churchill and Garbo really cut up some delicious touches. Sir Winston, it turned out, was a Garbo fan from the Year One. And Miss Garbo worshiped that lion of an Englishman. Garbo told him how much she had admired the newsreels she had seen in which Churchill had made those mighty speeches during World War II, defying the Nazis. Then Miss Garbo delighted Sir Winston and Onassis by giving an excellent imitation of Sir Winston saying, as he did, on taking power: "I have nothing to offer but blood, toil, tears and sweat."

Then the woman who seldom laughs laughed and said: "Sir Winston, in a way it is a shame you became a statesman. You would have been a magnificent actor."

As Randolph Churchill, Sir Winston's son, told me some years later, his father informed Miss Garbo that, in his youth, he had considered the stage, "but instead I went into politics—which, of course, is quite similar. A politician is, in good part, an actor, although he never gets to play alongside anyone as ravishing as Greta Garbo."

In the period after Mr. Onassis divorced Tina and before he began living steadily with Maria Callas, there was seldom a week during which he did not phone Greta

Garbo, and every year they were together for at least
one month. He did not live with Garbo. She was always a
"visitor" at one of his villas in France or Greece or aboard
the *Christina*. And she made sure everyone knew she was
merely a visitor.

Garbo is an enigma in such matters. For twenty-five
years her closest companion was George Schlee. Schlee
died, six years ago, in a room next to Garbo's in the Hotel
Crillon in Paris. Garbo and Mr. Schlee crossed the Atlantic many times together, but always in separate cabins.
On several occasions Schlee and Garbo were simultaneously Mr. Onassis' house guests.

Schlee was married to Valentina, the dress designer.
They lived in the same apartment house, on 52nd Street
and the East River, in New York, where Garbo lives.
Apparently Schlee spent more time with Miss Garbo than
with his wife, but *Time* magazine described Garbo's relations with Schlee and Valentina as "a very European
ménage à trois." On his visits to New York, Onassis often
took Schlee and Garbo out to dinner.

Ari and Garbo, without Schlee, were often seen together
browsing in the antique shops along Third Avenue or
looking at the animals in the zoo in Central Park. When
Maria Callas came so firmly into Ari's life, Garbo slowly
slipped away; Callas, the fiery Greek, was not Garbo's
cup of tea. And then—there is no question about it—
there was naked jealousy.

I have no way of knowing if Aristotle Onassis ever
loved Greta Garbo. More than likely, he loved her image,
and he loved playing the masculine role of guardian of
the mighty.

Did Garbo love Onassis? The Greek-born Naya Tolischus, who has known Onassis for ages—these days he

often drops into her New York restaurant, the Athena East—recalls a birthday party Ari gave for Garbo on the *Christina.* "When Mr. Onassis insisted that Garbo cut the cake," she told me, "Garbo was like a child. The way she looked at him. If I hadn't already known it, I would have known it then and there. Garbo loved him very much."

Ari's longest-enduring romance, before his marriage to the former Mrs. Kennedy, was with Maria Callas, a New York-born Greek who could sing like an angel, swear like a dockwalloper, and, according to her many admirers, kiss as if she were resuscitating a drowning man.

Ari met Miss Callas at a party in Venice and they had a long, moonlit gondola ride together, and things were never again the same. Miss Callas was then at the height of her vocal powers, hailed by her claque as "the female Caruso." She had them standing in the aisles from La Scala to New York's Met, and she was forever tardy when it came to keeping engagements; *impossible! temperamental! prima donna!*

At the time, Miss Callas was married to an elderly Milan businessman, Battista Meneghini, who also managed her affairs. (Miss Callas' opinion of Mr. Meneghini's managerial capabilities was voiced, some years later, after Ari married Jackie, with this characteristic blast and lament: "There have been two men in my life. The first took all my money. The second broke my heart.")

After Miss Callas divorced her Milanese, she and Ari became closer than Abercrombie and Fitch, jetting here, dancing there, dining everywhere. They shared the Avenue Foch apartment in Paris and the villa at Glyfada, and she was permanently on the *Christina's* passenger list. During the years they were together Ari gave the opera star jewels, securities, and a one-third interest in a tanker—all told worth around $1,000,000. Since he married Jackie it is understood he sent Miss Callas, among other things, a check for $50,000.

From time to time, when Ari is in Paris without Jackie, he and Miss Callas take tea or dinner, although often their meetings wind up in a sharp exchange of swear words in Greek, French, or English, whatever is the mood. However, Miss Callas makes no bones about how she felt and still feels about him.

"Onassis was my true love. Even today he is my best friend," she said recently. "I am sure that the friendship, in spite of the break that has occurred between us, will never end. And if I can say that with confidence it is because I know myself well and I know Aristotle well. His marriage changes nothing."

Then Miss Callas, showing her pretty little teeth, added: "I am happy if he is happy, even with another woman. There is only one queston to which none of us can give an answer. Is he happy with a woman who is always known by the name of her previous husband—Jacqueline Kennedy? We have our own feelings about that. But the future will tell us."

Whatever the future will tell us about Jackie and Ari, we can be sure that not even the infirmities of age will stop him from wandering across the face of the earth in behalf of profit and romance. Mr. Onassis' compulsion, as a twentieth-century Argonaut, is a very Greek compulsion. He is not the only citizen of the original democracy to achieve such great successes in business and with women.

In fact, there are two hundred and fifty self-made, Greek-born multimillionaires who have made their fortunes in shipping and whose hobby, like Mr. Onassis', is spending their money on the women they love. The wives and girl friends of these Golden Greeks are mankind's most pampered females.

Chapter Eleven

GIRLS OF THE GOLDEN GREEKS

Since she married Aristotle Onassis, the former Mrs. Kennedy has come to know many other Greek shipping magnates and their fortunate wives. Jackie, who never in her life was strapped for a buck, has been flabbergasted. "If you want to be happy," she told a friend in Paris last fall, "marry a Greek—a rich Greek."

As Jackie loves to tell her non-Greek pals, the life style of her husband and the other Golden Greeks is something else again from the American multimillionaires she has known, like the Rockefellers, duPonts, and Kennedys, who also can spend a few hundred million dollars and still have enough left over for a light lunch.

Jackie is well aware that the American super-rich, concerned with their image, try to give the impression that they live moderately. Being ostentatious, flaunting one's wealth—well, in this country it simply isn't done.

That attitude is a joke to Golden Greeks, Onassis very much included. Unlike rich Americans, who hide their private pleasures as if they were military secrets, the Greeks are extroverts plain and simple. They know that money doesn't necessarily buy happiness—but it doesn't necessarily buy *un*happiness, either.

Stephanos Zotos, author of *The Greeks*, who has been writing about Onassis and other shippers for thirty years, told me: "Mr. Onassis, like the wealthy Greeks of antiquity, is a sensualist, but he is not necessarily mean, and he has a good conscience. For him there is no sin in the pleasure of the sexes. He loves women and wine as much as his ancestors did. He does not practice moderation, but boasts about his pleasures."

Now that Jackie is herself a Girl of the Golden Greeks, let us check out her new pals and see how they spend their money. . . .

A good description of the golden way of life was once given by the late Eugenie Livanos, the sister of Tina, Onassis' first wife. When Eugenie was married to Onassis' bitter personal and business rival, Stavros Niarchos, who is rated in the half-billion-dollar class, she said: "Whenever we see anything beautiful we buy it. Once we have furnished a house or an apartment [she had ten in five countries] we rarely change it around. How can we? We never stay any place long enough to get bored with our surroundings."

Niarchos once bought Eugenie the entire art collection of actor Edward G. Robinson, for $3,000,000. At the time of the acquisition a friend asked Niarchos:

"How come, Stavros, this sudden interest in art?"

Niarchos shrugged and said: "Ah, well, my wife wanted to have some pretty pictures around the place."

Another example of the golden life can be found in the domestic routine of Costas Lemos, who owns Triton Shipping. One night, a few years ago, Lemos and his wife were dining in their New York apartment when she said: "You know, darling, this place needs a little touching up." "Why not?" said Mr. Lemos, and that was that.

So Mrs. Lemos called in a decorator and gave him carte blanche. The "little touching up" eventually came to $500,000.

Another Greek shipowner, one fine April-in-Paris day, was strolling with his girl friend of ten days down the Champs Elysées. She paused to admire a creamy, dreamy $23,000 Rolls-Royce in a dealer's showroom and—*pow!* —thirty minutes later she was behind the wheel and the certificate of ownership was in her purse.

Another lucky girl is Elli Goulandris. For one thing, from the time she was old enough to join the Girl Scouts she was a great beauty. For another thing, she happened to be working as a manicurist in a shop when shipowner Basil Goulandris walked in to have his nails done.

Basil was hooked out of his mind. Overnight Elli did the Cinderella bit—from rags to Givenchy gowns. To prove that he cared, Basil bought her, shortly after the marriage, an original Gauguin. Titled "Still Life With Apples and Flowers," it cost him $290,000.

Aristotle Onassis learned a thing or two about Greek wedding gifts, which perhaps should be called "dowries," when he married Tina, whose father, Stavros, owned eighty-odd ships outright. One of Stavros' presents to the couple was a Liberty ship worth $500,000.

Pericles Callimanupolous, head of Hellenic Lines, is said to have given a mere niece, the day she got married, a check for $100,000, which helped the newlyweds make a down payment on a vacuum cleaner.

The Golden Greeks, born dirt-poor, had no time for play in their early years and they didn't strike big gold until they were in their forties. Few of them married until they passed forty, and usually they married much younger women.

Stavros Livanos was more than twenty years his wife's senior. Niarchos married Eugenie Livanos when she was eighteen and he was thirty-eight—twenty years difference. Onassis married Tina Livanos when she was seventeen and he was forty—twenty-three years difference. Also, there's at least twenty-three years difference between Onassis and the former Mrs. Kennedy. The Golden Greeks have discovered one way to bridge the generation gap. With money.

Like Onassis, all the Golden Greeks have wives who are forever in orbit, jetting here and there, and they prefer having their own places to stay in on two, and sometimes three, continents. One such restless lady is Dolly Goulandris, the wife of Nicholas Goulandris, one of the Orion shipping clan.

Dolly and Nicholas own so many fantastic mansions they could spend each month of the year at a different one. For instance, if January gets chilly in London, Dolly, a smashing brunette, closes down her flat there and packs the poodles, Daisy and Bobo, and flies to her villa, "Olympiakos," in Nassau. "Olympiakos" has been described by no less an authority than *Vogue* as "a gem, a frame, a case that encloses and defines the special Island in the Sun kind of life."

Besides the main house there's a separate two-bedroom

minivilla for VIP guests with an ever-ready butler to unpack your shaving kit—or your extra living bra.

When asked about the size of the "Olympiakos" swimming pool, a socialite visitor told me: "A school of whales would not feel cramped." Adjacent to the pool there's a canopied terrace, a sheltered spot for luncheon that turns into Mrs. Goulandris' private nightclub after dark, complete with orchestra and entertainers.

Mrs. Goulandris says: "For me the summer belongs to Greece." In Athens she has a gigantic duplex, with a priceless collection of Cycladic art, including statues, out of ancient Greece. The apartment is just across the street from the Royal Palace, and Mrs. Goulandris used to drop over, maybe to borrow a cup of sugar from her old friend Queen Frederika. Alas, not any more. Nowadays, royalty is not a growth stock, and the Queen is in exile in Rome.

Furthermore, Mrs. Goulandris has villas on *three* different Greek islands. Her favorite is Skyros, a fair sail from Skorpios, which is being called "The Ionian Hyannis Port" these days.

Skyros is, to some extent, primarily a dock-site for the 108-foot-long Goulandris yacht, *Vagrant*. (Another Golden Greek, who has *four* yachts, said: "Nicholas Goulandris has only one yacht; still, he and his wife seem happy.")

It is interesting to see that among those listed in the current *New York Social Register* are Mr. and Mrs. Aristotle Socrates Onassis and other Golden Greeks. It was not always thus. Early in 1960, proper Bostonian Cleveland Amory, who makes a profession of such things, polled long-established socialites on "Who Killed Society?" Among those blamed were "The Kennedy Family" and "Aristotle Onassis."

The Old Guard disliked the Kennedys and Onassis, because they were "pushy" and did not come over on the *Mayflower*. But Jacqueline Bouvier was born into the Social Register, unlike John Kennedy and Aristotle Onassis. She never had to be pushy; she had all the essential credentials, and the manners. But most of the other Girls of the Golden Greeks, before they could show themselves in the better living rooms, had some brushing up to do. But all that is ancient history. Today the Kennedys and the Golden Greeks are welcome any place. Not long ago the British photographer-designer Cecil Beaton told a friend: "Today international society has a Greek accent." It's true. Thanks to the tourist attraction that is Jacqueline Onassis, the crème de la crème were table-to-table last summer in Athens zesty cafés, clutching Greek grammars as fiercely as Chinese clutching the collected sayings of Chairman Mao. And you should have seen Piraeus. There were so many yachts anchored helter-skelter in non-anchoring areas that the harbor police, it was rumored, considered a yacht towaway program.

Just who is who in international society? Lucy Kavaler, an American authority on old blue blood and new green currency, observes: "I find it dominated by the figures of the Duke and Duchess of Windsor, Colonel Serge Obolensky, Princess Grace of Monaco, and the Greek shipowners, Aristotle Onassis, Basil Goulandris (and his brothers), and Stavros Niarchos."

The new Greek aristocracy live in a manner of regal, wandering supersplendor, but generally their private lives are remarkably free of scandal, except for a divorce here and there. However, some of the Golden Greeks and the international jet set they dominate, are pretty kinky; they

seem determined to spend their millions strictly on pleasures of the flesh, orgies, stuff like that.

Shortly before he died, America's number one society
columnist, Maury Paul ("Cholly Knickerbocker"), made
the definitive comment when he said: "In international
society nobody gives a damn who you sleep with. What
is important is who you're seen with."

There's a popular story about one Greek shipping owner
who didn't even care who he was seen with. On his
silver wedding anniversary he gave a jolly dinner party
at Maxim's in Paris, and made the seating arrangements
himself. On his right sat his wife, on his left his mistress.

Cleveland Amory says of the jet set: "Relations between
the sexes are so complicated that the only way you can
tell if members of the set are going together is if they're
married. Then, almost certainly, they're not."

You can make it in the Greek jet set, even without an
enormous bankroll, if you're talented, like Leonard Bernstein, Margot Fonteyn, Salvador Dali, or the Rolling
Stones. If you're very beautiful—male or female—you're
also welcome, and you can be a permanent house guest.

A wealthy Greek widower, considerably advanced in
years, was once asked why he always had his guest rooms
occupied by attractive young things. "I like to be surrounded," he said, "by beautiful pictures and beautiful
furniture. What's more beautiful than beautiful youth?"

The whole jet set seems designed by the Goddess of
Love. Temptation is everywhere. The late Ludwig Bemelmans, one of the Greeks' favorite artists—he decorated
the nursery on the *Christina*—once said: "At a Greek
party sex is passed around like salted peanuts at a middle-
class cocktail party."

No self-respecting Greek millionairess would give a

party without inviting good-looking extra young men and women. The young people are expected to help out, raise morale. You know, flatter an aging tycoon into thinking he's Tom Jones. And flatter old ladies into forgetting their steel-reinforced girdles.

On occasion, jet set parties serve worthy causes. One afternoon two summers ago, at a Greek millionaire's villa near Antibes, the guests were lolling around the massive lapis-lazuli swimming pool when the hostess had a sudden inspiration. "All the young people," she cried, "get into the swimming pool."

After they obliged, she addressed herself to the oldsters outside the pool. "Now, I'll be the auctioneer," she said. "And I want you to bid—for your favorite charity—for the youngsters' bathing suits."

A young lady's bikini brought $500 for the American Red Cross. A young man's trunks brought £100 for the British Royal Society for the Prevention of Cruelty to Animals. What fun! When a boy or girl was successfully bid for, he or she climbed out of the pool, naked as a peeled banana, and holding suit in hand, delivered it to the highest bidder.

These beautiful young people, of course, get free food and lodging, but they are also rewarded in other ways. Stavros Niarchos often gives his guests solid gold cigarette boxes. Mrs. Marcos Nomikos—her husband is another shipping magnate—one time gave a Chinese dinner on her yacht. When the guests opened their fortune cookies they found, instead of clever little predictions, bills in denominations of $50 and $100.

Then, for the attractive, ambitious girl, there's a chance to meet movie moguls like Darryl Zanuck and Sam Spiegel, who often attend Golden Greek parties. Who knows—a girl might be discovered; so might a boy. A staggeringly handsome young Italian—he reminded one lady of Michelangelo's "David"—was discovered at a party a few years ago, but in a different way. Being, as Noel Coward once said, "high-spirited, like all Italians," he became the permanent house guest of a wealthy Greek shipping widow who introduced him, just to make things right, as "my nephew." Insiders accepted the deception with good grace, although they were amused to recall her "nephews" of previous years. One, a novice bullfighter, she met while taking the sun in Málaga. Another, a straw-blond German, she met while taking the waters in Baden-Baden. A third, a husky, hawk-nosed Arab, she met while taking lunch on the fabulous terrace of the Hotel St. Georges in Beirut. He was the bus boy working her table.

To explain their lack of concern about private lives, the cosmopolitan Greek hostesses are fond of quoting that ever-quotable British actress, Mrs. Patrick Campbell. Years before the automobile was popular, Mrs. Campbell, discussing morals, said: "I don't care what people do, as long as they don't do it in the streets and frighten the horses."

The restless wandering of the modern Argonauts across the face of the earth, seeking riches and romance, is a peculiarly Greek story. Their success in romance is attributable to the fact that they first succeeded in making money. But this is denied by the Greeks themselves as an insult to a virile race. A vigorous defense of the Greek male's romantic abilities, with or *without* money, has been made by my colleague, Stephanos Zotos, the Greek journalist and novelist.

"From Pericles to Onassis," wrote Mr. Zotos in *McCalls*

magazine, "from Odysseus to Prince Philip, and from Paris to Constantine, there has been a steady sequence of incredible romantic adventures, which have established a legend about Greek manhood. Long before Aristotle and Jacqueline, there was the famed romance between Eugénie, Empress of French (1853-71), consort of Napoleon III, and her Greek doctor, Andonios Chrystomanos.

"The actress Sarah Bernhardt became a helpless toy in the hands of a Greek, Jacques Damala, an attaché of the Greek diplomatic corps in Paris, a notorious Don Juan, described as a combination Casanova and Marquis de Sade. In modern times, a daughter of Charles Chaplin's went to Athens on a quick visit, only to fall deeply in love with the heir of prominent Greek fur merchants.

"Young Charlotte Ford found herself unable to resist the charm of Stavros Niarchos, the rival shipowner of Onassis, and married him though she was many years his junior. At the end of a successful career, French songstress Edith Piaf lost her head over a very young Greek barber, whom she named Theo Sarapo.

"Every Greek man is absolutely convinced he is the only man who can chart the entire world. This belief gives him assurance and audacity, two qualities that attract women.

"The history of ancient Greece provides a barely tenable but highly quotable reason for the reputation Greek men enjoy today. It is known that mothers in the martial state of Sparta would climb the summit of Mt. Taygetus to throw to their death those of their newborn sons who did not seem to meet the strict requirements of manhood.

"The tall, blonde Swedish girls who troop to Greece (these days) in summer are said to be not nearly as much interested in visiting the ancient ruins as they are eager to find the company of Greek escorts, Middle-aged women from various parts of the world seem determined to have one last fling along the sunny beaches of Greece or in the shadow of an ancient pillar."

Because he is himself a Greek, Mr. Zotos, of course, cannot be expected to be entirely objective. All of the Greeks can't be Casanovas, and some of their women must be influenced by their husbands' willingness to practically swamp them with goodies and to make it possible for them to be ever on the run, from one international playground to another.

What normal female, for example, would not put her soul in hock to enjoy the luxurious global jettings that have made Jackie Onassis' years with Ari a moveable feast?

PART FOUR

The
Swinging
Life

Chapter Twelve

A MOVEABLE FEAST

Ernest Hemingway, who used the above title, once said: "One who can spontaneously travel, de luxe class, accompanied by competent servants to do the drab, daily details, has achieved the ultimate in human freedom."

Hemingway could have been talking about Jackie Onassis. For example, one day in March of 1969, Jackie, in her Fifth Avenue apartment, was talking on the telephone to Aristotle, who was in Athens trying to wrap up a $400,000,000 deal with the ruling military junta. He said the negotiations were on ice, for the moment; he had some free time, and would she like to get together? (In Jackie's set, the men *are* different. They phone their wives for a date.)

Jackie said swell, New York is like the South Pole, why

don't we meet someplace where it's warm? Onassis said how about the Canary Islands? That was fine with Jackie; it had been a good two months since she had been outside the United States. They arranged to meet in Las Palmas, the capital of the Canary Islands, eight days later. Jackie decided to make a couple of stops en route, so after saying good-bye to Caroline and John, Jr., she took off for Paris on a Pan American jet, accompanied by her maid and her ever-present bodyguard. They bought four first-class seats—one for the maid, one for the bodyguard, and two for Jackie, so she could take a proper nap. In one of her valises were bed linen and towels, just in case the former First Lady had to spend a night in a hotel.

That wasn't necessary in Paris, where Jackie stayed at their fifth-floor apartment on tree-lined Avenue Foch, an apartment with seventeenth-century paneling and with paintings that, if auctioned at Parke-Bernet's in New York or Sotheby's in London, would bring a cool $1,000,-000, if not more.

For a few days in Paris, Jackie visited with old friends, including the then U.S. Ambassador, Sargent Shriver, who is married to a Kennedy. She lunched and dined at such places of *haute cuisine* as Maxim's (dinner for two averages $60), where you can get your arm broken by ordering a cheeseburger. Jackie stopped at several dress houses, and had her hair done at Alexandre's by Alexandre himself, with his golden scissors. His clients include Maria Callas, who was not present at the time; things being what they are, that was just as well.

Jackie nipped around town in one of Ari's three Paris-based vehicles, a chauffeur-driven Rolls-Royce, specially upholstered, air-conditioned, and with a compact bar and ice machine in the rear to help pass the time during traffic jams. One of Mrs. Onassis' French friends heard she was in town and phoned. She was told Jackie was driving downtown; she could phone the car, and was given the number. The chauffeur answered, and when she asked for Mrs. Onassis, he said: "I'm sorry, Mrs. Onassis is on the other phone."

After a couple of days in Paris, Jackie flew to Switzerland, where she visited her then-ailing sister, Lee Radziwill; then off to the Canary Islands and the *Christina*.

The yacht used to be the Canadian frigate *Stormont*. However, sailors who served on the *Stormont* would hardly have recognized her. The Canadian navy, though ever considerate of its men's comforts, never would have authorized the marble bidets, not to mention the mosaic dance floor that drops down to become a swimming pool, the first-rate wine cellar, and the motor launch with special tow ropes for water skiing.

Jackie occupies the master two-room suite, which is almost roomy enough for Broadway Joe Namath to unload the "bomb." The bedroom is a replica of one in King Minos' palace at Knossos. The fixtures, which have gold fish-mouth taps, are made from Siena marble. When Jackie first saw the huge kidney-shaped bathtub, when she inspected the *Christina* with the then Senator John Kennedy some years ago, she exclaimed: "Why, it's large enough for a carrier of the *Forrestal* class!"

For eight days the *Christina* moved around the high seas as if it were on a secret mission. If all the conflicting press reports about her movements were taken seriously, the yacht would have been simultaneously traveling north, south, east, and west. According to a member of the crew, Aristotle spent several hours each day in his office, juggling his international empire and speaking to his agents around the world on the elaborate microwave radio setup.

Wearing one of the four pairs of Italian-style jeans she had picked up in the fall at Veneziano's in New York, Jackie spent hours in a deck chair teaching herself Greek and Greek history from books she ordered at Eleftheroudakis Brothers, Athens. (A few months ago, Jackie walked into her husband's Athens office and spoke to his secretary in suprisingly passable Greek. "Good morning," said Mrs. Onassis in Greek. "How are you? It's indeed very hot now in Athens." The secretary was as startled as if Lassie had walked in reciting the Gettysburg Address.)

Jackie also relaxed with detective stories; Ari isn't much of a reader. One time his rival, Stavros Niarchos, snorted: "The only thing Onassis ever reads are bank books."

After dining together, tête-à-tête, every evening, the Onassises had a movie shown in their private projection room. One night it was *The Magus*. After eight days underway, the *Christina*, white as a wedding cake, steamed majestically into Trinidad. It was reported in the local press that an excited port official, who spotted the ship through his long glass, phoned his superior and babbled: "It's here. The golden yacht. You know, the one that belongs to the Greek Kennedy."

Spontaneous travels, like the Canary Islands caper, took Jackie across the ocean, by sea and air, twelve times in the first year of her new marriage. Onassis, of course, practically commutes. Because he moves without advance notice, every night his beds in Paris and London, and in his Greek villa, are turned down, just to be on the safe side.

Since they were married, Mr. Onassis has purchased

for his wife, himself, her children, his children, relations, non-business friends, bodyguards, secretaries, and servants about seventy first-class round trip tickets from New York to Athens at $1,145 per or a total of $80,150. Airline travel inside Europe and the United States, plus hotels, gratuities, and sightseeing for themselves and their entourage, tapped Ari's wallet for around another $97,850. Thus the sum for moving hither and thither when *not* moving on the *Christina* rounds out at about $178,000.

When Jackie and Ari jet together, even the shortest hop is a regal cavalcade. After one of their periodic stopovers in Paris in June, 1969, the Onassises went to Nice (where the *Christina* was anchored) on one of Ari's private jets. The day before, their luggage, which included thirteen bags, plus hatboxes and Jackie's specially constructed leather cosmetic kit, large enough to keep an Indian tribe in war paint for a month, went by road in a truck. The truck was preceded by one of Mr. Onassis' limousines. The car was standing by at the airport when their plane landed. It really is hard, these days, to get a taxi, even on the Riviera.

This perpetual motion delights Jackie. It sounds exhausting, and it would be *if* she had to scurry about making reservations for proper transport and packing things and paying hotel bills. But Jackie is spared such tedious activities. Wherever she is, there's always one of those competent, completely anonymous women lurking in the shadows; called "private" or "social" secretaries, they earn $20,000 or $25,000 a year and are worth every cent. All Jackie has to do is say: "Rome. Tuesday. After lunch." Miss Anonymous zips into action. Jackie will be taken to the airport, ticketed, her shot record will be presented to the authorities, she will be tucked into her seat, and Miss Anonymous will hand the plane's steward a jar of caviar to place in the refrigerator and to serve as Jackie's pre-lunch snack. At Rome, Jackie will be met by another Miss Anonymous; no worries, no mixups, no delays.

For every trip Mr. and Mrs. Onassis make together they make at least two separately. During the first year of their marriage Jackie and Ari saw each other only 225 days. They were oceans apart 140 days.

Mr. Onassis made it very clear when he first married Jacqueline Kennedy that he had no intention of practicing family "togetherness." Shortly after they were married, he spelled out just what kind of a marriage this would be.

"Jackie is a little bird," he said, "that needs its freedom as well as its security, and she gets them both from me. She can do exactly as she pleases, visit international fashion shows and travel and go out with friends to the theater or any place. And I, of course, will do exactly as I please. I never question her and she never questions me."

Jackie and Ari's "separate but equal" status became public knowledge even during the first twelve days of their marriage, when Mr. Onassis took off for three days —leaving Jackie alone on Skorpios—to attend to a few hundred millions dollars worth of business. In the second month of their marriage, Jackie and Ari were together only eighteen days. Jackie left Skorpios on her own and flew to visit her sister Lee in London. Ari flew alone to Paris, where he went to a party that listed, among its other guests, Maria Callas. Ari made the nightclub rounds, then flew to London for a few days with Jackie, then back to Paris. Later, Jackie flew alone to New York. (One headline read: THE BRIDE COMES HOME *ALONE*.)

Ari outflies Jackie two to one, and he moves so fast and so continually Jackie isn't sure, from hour to hour, just where her husband is. One morning in New York a friend of hers telephoned and asked her, good-naturedly, what country Mr. Onassis was in this day.

"I don't know," Jackie replied. "But I'll probably know by dinner time. That's when he usually phones."

If you think the miles Jackie logged during the first year of her new marriage were simply a newlywed's last frivolity before settling down to the life of a homebody, hold everything! Just recently Mr. Onassis said: "We've been spending more time in Greece than we expect to in the future. Jackie will be doing lots of traveling." Ari was asked if he and Jackie will follow the jet-set route, a path he always trod in the past, and he said there was no doubt about it. After all, travel is what the jet set is all about. So, if you want to know where Jackie will probably be in the years ahead, study the jet set's migrations, which are governed, like those of the meadowlark, the yak, the Berber herdsman and the bobsledder, the sockeye salmon and the sea turtle, the lemming and the locust, by the eternal turning of the seasons:

Winter. It's Nassau and the Bahamas, to get tanned all day and fried all night, then on to the Swiss and Austrian ski slopes. The Springs—Palm, Colorado, and White Sulphur—still have their adherents, and Sun Valley is occasionally mentioned in Suzy's newspaper column.

The Onassises do not ignore Palm Beach, though it's a bit staid; you know, ancients in blazers and white flannels at the Everglades Club still cursing Franklin D. Roosevelt. They were there for a few days in 1969, but—horrors!—they had to anchor the *Christina* in unfashionable Miami —the yacht is simply too big to be accommodated in Palm

Beach. Among Palm Beach's regular winter visitors are Ari's old friends, the Duke and Duchess of Windsor, who come from New York by train; they refuse to fly.

Old Palm Beach hands recall, with shivers, the season that the Windsors, at the last minute, decided to skip Palm Beach and went, instead, to Tucson, Arizona, of all places. The dowager who had planned the dinner party of the season in the Windsors' honor—the invitations had already been mailed—took to her bed under medical supervision and was practically stuffed with tranquilizers.

In Palm Beach the Onassises are often house guests. But further south, in Nassau, they live aboard the *Christina*, though, at last report, Ari was looking at a $750,000 villa that had caught Jackie's eye. Jet setters without their own Nassau pads or yachts must throw themselves on the mercy of innkeepers who maintain clubby resorts, like the Coral Harbour at the tip of New Providence, which admits a hundred guests—by invitation only. Fort Knox is easier to crash.

In the Bahamas it's costly Paradise Island, where Ari loves to walk along the empty beaches, with his trousers rolled up and carrying his shoes in his hand, all alone, thinking and plotting Lord knows what. After visiting Paradise Island last year, a guest, commenting on the affluent atmosphere, said: "I dropped a half-dollar in the lobby and a fast bellhop picked it up. I had to tip him a dollar."

In February so many shipping men crowd St. Moritz's Palace Hotel that it's called "the Greek Grossinger's." Jet setters gather at the Corviglia Ski Club to read the latest casualty lists, and trade gossip. For a long time the gossips chewed over the Pier-6 verbal brawls Onassis seemed to be forever having with the pugnacious Maria

Callas, but now St. Moritz's juiciest memory concerns
Stavros Niarchos. One year Niarchos arrived with his
new bride, Charlotte Ford, granddaughter of the original
Henry, on their honeymoon. The bride checked into the
Palace. The bridegroom stayed at his nearby chalet—
with his ex-wife Eugenie.

One winter Ari's then wife, Tina, Eugenie's sister, went
kerplunk on the major slope and broke a leg. That's par
for the course. Last winter so many rich Greeks took
tumbles at St. Moritz that a reporter wired his paper in
Athens: "An estimated one billion dollars worth of Greek
jet setters are now in traction."

St. Moritz jumps; champagne corks pop like a Western
shoot-out and amorous males are ever on safari. More
conservative friends of Mr. and Mrs. Onassis favor the
serenity of Gstaad's Palace Hotel, or Schloss Mittersill,
in the Austrian Alps, near Salzburg, where people have
the old-fashioned habit of sleeping in their own rooms.

Spring. It's Paris. Where else? The Beautiful People
(including the Onassises) are summoned to an annual
feast given by Baroness Paule de Rothschild in her gem
of an apartment on Rue Méchain, which has priceless
eighteenth-century wallpaper, Paul Klee paintings, and
a writing desk rimmed by a two-inch strip of solid silver.
The Rothschilds have separate homes—the Baron lives
alone on Avenue d'Iéna. This seemingly eccentric arrangement, characteristic of international society, should not
be taken at face value. The Rothschilds are very close. He
phones her first thing every morning.

Summer. June is for London—the suites at Claridge's
are booked years in advance. (Ari keeps his suite permanently.)

Everyone attends the races at Ascot, and after the

races the Beautiful People frequent the Clermont, the utmost in casinos, 44 Berkeley Square, where the nightingales sang. The Clermont attracts the shipping crowd and their bejeweled wives. There is an old saying: "If a Greek doesn't gamble, he's an Armenian."

After London, the social gypsies camp along the Mediterranean's southern coast, from Marseilles to the Greek islands, and the *Christina* is practically a ferryboat, hopping from port to port. While Greece is booming, the French Riviera is still where it's at. The July, 1969, opening of the aptly named Summer Sporting Club at Monte Carlo—the season's first bash—was dominated, as usual, by Princess Grace, in a long pink dress by Dior and a striped Mexican shawl. It seems as if every jet setter of importance was there—except the most important of them all, Mr. and Mrs. Aristotle Onassis. It is a shame, for Ari loves Monte Carlo, but he is still not welcome. In fact, last summer there was a slick bit of diplomatic knife-throwing by Prince Rainier and his lady, and the knife was thrown at Aristotle Onassis. The occasion was the prestigious annual Red Cross Gala, and who do you think shared the seat of honor at the right hand of Prince Rainier and had the privilege of the first dance with him? Maria Callas.

In August the fashionables congregate in Rome, where last year Jackie did some fierce shopping and attended a private showing of Antonio's fall creations. Nowadays in Rome, jet-set parties are held clandestinely, thanks to the respected Italian custom of concealing one's real income from the tax collector. If a Roman publicly expended his money on *la dolce vita*, snoopy collectors would descend on his books with a costly thump.

Mr. Onassis paid a courtesy call on the exiled Queen

Mother of Greece, Frederika. Queen Frederika, by the way, played a large part in persuading Ari to take over the nearly bankrupt Greek national airline, and turn it into money-making Olympic Airways.

Autumn. New York, of course. Where you can spend more money than anyplace else on earth—if you really try.

Chapter Thirteen

GO! GO! GO!

Except when they are on the high seas on the *Christina*, Mr. and Mrs. Onassis never spend an evening at home, just the two of them. You'd think, with all their super-pads and four-star private chefs, they'd want, at least once in a while, to put their feet up in front of the fireplace and maybe catch *Laugh-In* on television. But no. As soon as the sun goes down the Onassises get itchy, and presently they're off to restaurants and theaters and cafés and wherever else the action is. For Jackie and Ari Onassis, every night is New Year's Eve. Let us check out their nocturnal movements for one week in New York during the early fall of 1969.

Sunday. Jackie and Ari attended a late-afternoon screening of the naughty Swedish movie, *I am Curious (Yellow)*. After the show, Jackie, it is said, worked over a photographer as though she had a black belt in karate; more

about that later. Then they dined at La Seine, an establishment associated with the same man who operates the
fabulous Tour d'Argent in Paris, Claude Terrail. La Seine
is New York's newest and most elegant French restaurant.
It has its own art gallery of French impressionists which,
as long as we're talking about money, is valued at over
$1,000,000.

Monday. Jackie and Ari dined at "21," then went to
Raffles, the elegant private discothèque (membership:
$2,000 a year), with Mr. and Mrs. Charles Spaulding; he
was one of President Kennedy's old school chums. In their
honor Raffles spun Greek records, and Dimitri Kritas, the
Greek-born designer, won Jackie's applause when he did
an erotic, gymnastic dance of his homeland. An onlooker
described Mr. Kritsas' activities on the dance floor as being
"as wild as the fertility rites of Congo tribesmen."

Tuesday. The Onassises took their nourishment at La
Côte Basque. Then, since the evening was mild, they
started to stroll up Fifth Avenue and do some leisurely
window-shopping. But soon a crowd of rubberneckers was
following them and growing larger with every block.
Someone called police headquarters and said that a
demonstration of some sort was under way. Jackie and
Ari climbed into a limousine as sirens heralded the approach of the squad cars.

Wednesday. Ari dined with his daughter, Christina, at
Trader Vic's, while Jackie went with the David Altmans
to a Broadway preview of *Indians*, a show about Buffalo
Bill. After the show, the Altmans, who have the average
couple's need for an occasional breather, went straight
home. Not Jackie. Escorted by William vanden Heuvel,
an old Kennedy political crony, she went uptown to The
Ginger Man for white wine and cheeseburgers.

Thursday. Jackie and Ari dined at La Caravelle, a restaurant long believed to have been partially financed, at least, by Joseph P. Kennedy. You can often see one or more members of the Kennedy clan in the house. La Caravelle is equal in price range to another Onassis hangout, Le Pavillon, generally believed to be one of the most expensive restaurants in the world. Dinner for four can run over $400 if you order things like caviar, baby lamb, and 1949 Château Haut-Brion at $75 the magnum.

Friday. Ari broke bread with some business associates at "21," while Jackie went with Oliver Smith, the stage designer, to Elaine's, one of those chic Second Avenue bistros. Mrs. Onassis and Mr. Smith were practically dinosaurs at Elaine's, which caters to the issue of New York's most affluent; the clients consider anyone a day over thirty a senior citizen. Elaine is a celebrity in her own right, all two hundred pounds of her, and when she dances to a rock 'n' roll number, the joint shakes like an earthquake with a high rating on the Richter scale.

Saturday. Jackie and Ari were back at La Côte Basque again. Then again to Raffles, accompanied by George Plimpton, who writes best-selling books.

Besides dining in restaurants every night during this hectic week, Mr. and Mrs. Onassis had lunch out—separately—every day except Sunday. One afternoon Jackie took Caroline, John, Jr., three of their school chums, and two Secret Servicemen to Palisades Amusement Park, across the Hudson River in New Jersey. They ate hot dogs and drank Cokes and rode the roller coaster and the other scary things that kids insist on going on. Jackie, suffering an unusual attack of economy, bought a block of discount tickets for rides and eats, thus getting a free give-away bottle of Top Job household cleanser.

All this restaurant and nightclub hopping, as anyone who has gone out for as much as a ham sandwich in recent years knows, is a costly proposition, particularly when you're a chronic "I'll pay for it" type like Mr. Onassis. It is conservative to say that a week seldom passes when Ari and Jackie do not spend from $1,600 to $1,700 outside of their home on food and drinks and tips, tips, tips. That's a weekly average of $1,650, or an annual total of $85,860, which should make the Onassises the most popular citizens with restaurateurs since Diamond Jim Brady.

At none of the public houses mentioned above was Mr. Onassis asked to produce cash, a check, or a Diners' Club card. He was not even shown the check. His bills are sent to him at the end of each month, with twenty percent added for the waiter and ten percent for the captain. There is a certain reliance here on the integrity of the proprietor. However, in the long run, it would be unwise to try padding Mr. Onassis' bill; his memory bank is so efficient that he can remember, months later, exactly where he dined on a particular evening, with whom, and what he ate.

No one of logical mind wishes to lose such an easy-with-a-buck patron for a small crooked profit, but some establishments are just silly. Like a certain highly popular restaurant in Paris that is now shunned by Mr. Onassis as a cheat. Several years ago it billed him $154 for dinner for four. On the date of the bill Mr. Onassis had dined with friends in Palm Beach, Florida.

During the entire month of October, 1969, the only night Jackie and Ari stayed home for a meal was the night of the twentieth, when they gave a dinner party to mark their first wedding anniversary. It is understood that their regular French chef downed his cooking tools temporarily in indignation because Mr. Onassis imported, to supervise the spread, the chef from La Côte Basque.

Mr. Onassis talked his own chef into a more relaxed mood by pointing out that the man from La Côte Basque, although he was as French as a shrug, had had quite some experience with the preparation of lamb, in the Greek manner, which Ari dotes on. The main dish at the anniversary party was very young "milk" lamb—that is, the lamb was still feeding at his mother's breast when removed to the butcher shop on Madison Avenue, which charged Ari $50 per lamb. It took quite a number of these tiny "milk" lambs to feed Onassis' guests, who included Rose Kennedy, Mr. and Mrs. William Paley, and Leonard Bernstein, who nobly passed up an anti-Vietnam War rally to attend the party.

After dinner Ari presented Jackie with gifts of magnificent jewels. The guests were quietly sworn to secrecy—publicity about jewels does not elate Ari, who sees a thief behind every drape. However, it can be said that almost $500,000 in gems passed into Jackie's keeping that night. It was indeed a happy anniversary.

These days Jackie seems to be tireless. During her years in the White House she was somewhat of a party-pooper, forever begging off early, complaining of a headache or about the need for some sleep. Now she seldom comes home before the milkman.

Besides making the restaurant and nightclub circuit, Jackie and Ari each day receive dozens of invitations to almost every worthwhile social gathering in town. When they do show up, Jackie is the center of attention, and she accepts this as her due. Discussing Jackie and New York party-going, author George Carpozi, Jr., quoted an "old-line society matron, whose husband was one of President Kennedy's confidants," as saying:

"Many people, particularly women, hate it when Jackie comes to a party because she almost *demands* to be the center of attention. She is almost condescending to them. She has an air about her—an air of superiority that makes her look down on other women. She is sometimes rude and intrusive. But she does it in such a way that it looks to most people—specially to the men—that this surge of attention is spontaneous and not her own doing."

Then the matron went on to decry Jackie's habit of "borrowing" other women's husbands as escorts when Ari is out of town. "If I threw myself the way she does at Leonard Bernstein, and others," she said, "I'd be accused of trying to take them away from their wives. But Jackie does it all so expertly and smoothly, hardly anyone notices. Not even poor Leonard's wife. I know if my husband went squiring Jackie, I'd break his head open."

People who are encountering Jackie for the first time in New York have found (what Washingtonians have long known) that Jackie changes her mind more often than a child trying to decide how to spend a dime in a candy store. Particularly about people.

When Jackie first appeared on the New York scene, for example, she paid some attention to Andy Warhol and the pop art crowd. Andy and his satellites figured that, having been recognized by Mrs. Onassis, the friendship would be forever. But this was not to be. After accepting a few of their invitations, Jackie quickly tired of them and totally ignored them. And it wasn't only the Warhol Rat Pack that quickly bored Jackie. One frankly furious New York hostess said of herself and her world-famous husband: "She picked us up, squeezed us to pieces, then dropped us like hot potatoes. She gets crushes on people, but they don't last for long."

Another of the groups Jackie has gradually tired of are those intellectuals who so long served the late President. Arthur Schlesinger, Jr., is great fun if one is in a mood to discuss the Emancipation Proclamation, but that was not the subject foremost on Jackie's mind the night the historian took her to dine at Le Pavillon, when Ari was away. A captain at the restaurant, who kept his eyes on them, said: "Mr. Schlesinger talked and talked and Mrs. Kennedy looked as if she wished she was ten thousand miles away."

Of the New Frontiersmen, Jackie herself has said, laughing: "I don't understand a word they say."

Hurt, the Kennedy partisans have struck back. Said Jim Bishop, author of *The Day Kennedy Was Shot:* "If she is an intellectual, it does not show. . . . At best she is an attractive, selfish child. She finds it simple to divide people between *us* and *them.* She has the snob's consciousness of *our* set."

While Jackie and Ari occasionally give an intimate sit-down dinner party in their Fifth Avenue apartment, or in their apartment on Avenue Foch in Paris—and they're forever taking people out to lunch or dinner—they do most of their serious entertaining in Greece, on the *Christina,* or in the jumping native tavernas that have captivated Jackie.

Every time Mr. Onassis tosses a party (and Jackie leaves that to him) it is a lavish affair. Dean Martin, once a happy Onassis house guest, says: "Ari doesn't give a party, he produces one. He is the Joseph E. Levine of party giving."

Ari thinks nothing of flying as many as fifty to a hundred guests from Athens in one of his private sea or land planes or helicopters. They land on the airstrip near the Skorpios villa, or in the water alongside the *Christina*. Also airlifted from the mainland are orchestras, entertainers, foodstuffs, and wines.

One thing that incenses Jackie is that every time they throw a party, despite all their security precautions, it winds up on Page One. (Jackie sorely misses the gentler era, when she was a girl, when it was believed, that "a lady's name should be in the paper three times. When she is born, when she marries, and when she dies.")

One night in 1968, a most discreet group of friends were flown to the *Christina*, together with a band that had been sworn, by one of Mrs. Onassis' secretaries, to utter secrecy. But, alas, such is the nature of man when the great are involved that, a few days later, one of the musicians, one Yahnis Poulopoulis, held what was practically a press conference at the bar of one of the busiest hotels in Athens. "We, the musicians, wore tuxedos," he said, "while the guests were very, very informal. Jackie Onassis asked for some Greek folk songs. Very soon Mr. Onassis, some English show people, and some Greek and Swedish girls were dancing the *Spyrtaki*. The party was still going on at dawn, when Jackie and Princess Radziwill put on bikinis and jumped into the water."

Naturally, the Athens papers headlined the affair: *BIKINI PARTY ON SKORPIOS*.

Mr. Poulopoulis did say one thing to the press that pleased Ari. He admitted that he and the other musicians had been amply rewarded for their services. This is always the way; no one who pleases Jackie or Ari ever has cause to complain about the pay. For example, last year Jackie became fascinated with the bearded Greek singer Stamatis Kokotas, when she heard him belt out both *bouzouki* songs and modern hits at a *taverna*. Mr. Onassis, on Jackie's suggestion, put into Mr. Kokotas' palm a crisp $100 bill.

After that night, every few days Mr. Kokotas would be flown to Skorpios, with his accordion, to sing during dinner, even if Jackie and Ari had no guests. Kokotas was always paid $500 for a few hours' work, and while that is not overwhelming by Las Vegas standards, it is, for the average Greek, five months' pay.

One evening Kokotas was summoned to the *Christina* by Jackie when Mr. Onassis was away. On his arrival he was told that Jackie had decided to dine alone in her cabin, but that he should set himself up on the deck and she would hear him through the porthole. (Jackie's desire to hear but not to see the entertainer that night may be compared, by social historians, with the conduct of the Boston heiress Mrs. Jack Gardner some years ago. Mrs. Gardner paid the pianist Paderewski $3,000 to play at tea-time for an elderly friend and herself, on condition that he remain concealed behind a screen.)

Flying guests and others around, in order to give a party the proper mix, is nothing new for Mr. Onassis. In fact, judging by some of the things he has done in the past, the flight from Athens to Skorpios is like a short taxi ride. Some years ago, when he owned a fleet of whaling ships, he and a group of his friends were sitting around Paris, fighting a losing battle against boredom. Ari, who could always be depended on in a crisis, had a sudden inspiration. He enlisted twelve male fun-seekers, hired a commercial passenger plane, and flew them down to Lima. The Onassis whaling fleet was, at that time, fishing off the Peruvian coast. Ari's guests no more than had a chance to catch their breath in a Lima hotel, after the exhausting trip, when Ari took them out to one of his ships by helicopter. They spent two weeks, with harpoons in their hands, fishing for the valuable sperm whale, a treat seldom given even the most worldly jet setter.

Aristotle Onassis gambles his reputation every time he entertains. Boredom will not be tolerated. A while back one of Ari's friends, Anita Vanderbilt's son, Peter Howard, long a high flier, had this comment to make on proper fun. "Giving a successful party," said Mr. Howard, "is like mixing a successful salad, a matter of proportions. One invites a writer (Truman Capote), a Duke (Windsor), a Greek multimillionaire shipping man (Onassis), a couple of dancers from a long-run show (*Hello Dolly*), some stuffy, wealthy socialites, and a brace of hippies."

Mr. Howard himself once entertained in a Roman nightclub, in honor of Anita Ekberg and Linda Christian, so successfully that he was condemned by the Vatican and expelled from Italy. The morning after the party, the cleaners found an evening gown in the powder room.

During their $20,000,000 honeymoon, the Onassises spent, entertaining on the yacht or at one of their apartments or houses, what a specialist on feeding and amusing the very rich estimates to be $105,000. Jackie can now claim from Perle Mesta the title that that Washington hostess so long enjoyed: The Hostess With the Mostest.

When Jackie was Mrs. John F. Kennedy, she couldn't very well send her guests off whale fishing, but she did have the White House going for her. She certainly put her mark on entertaining in the Executive Mansion, although sometimes her desire to bring the old place "into the twentieth century" bombed. For instance, Jackie did away with the formal receiving line and everyone kind of stood around trying to make conversation, as if they were at a cocktail party, while the President and the First Lady walked around informally, trying to say hello to as many people as possible. Some guests, who weren't pushy enough, didn't get to shake the President's hand, and many a feather was ruffled.

Also, this standing around, when as many as two thousand people were present, resulted in some ghastly bunching, which the traditional receiving line tends to avoid. At one crush the wife of Congressman Clem Miller fainted dead away. Her embarrassed husband said, while fanning his wife's unconscious face: "Don't worry, she's always pregnant."

At the Kennedy's first official White House party Jackie ordered hard liquor served, something that had not been done at official functions during the Eisenhower Administration. Furthermore, this party was held on a Sunday, and the W. C. T. U. and the Bible Belt sent up a cry of protest. The next day's pile of newspapers carried headlines such as: LIQUOR ON SUNDAY AT THE WHITE HOUSE DRAWS CRITICISM. And: NEVER ON SUNDAY AT JFK'S HOUSE, SAYS BAPTIST CONGRESSMAN.

Hard liquor at the official Kennedy parties also had, on occasion, a more personal effect. One evening a white-tied young attaché from one of the Scandinavian embassies, who had drunk more than he should have, stepped smartly down the steps toward his taxi on the way home, and somehow fell into a hedge in full view of the entire diplomatic corps. The last time anybody heard about him it was said that he had been posted, in a minor capacity, to Nairobi.

Despite such setbacks here and there, Betty Beale, society columnist for the Washington *Star*, was among those who thought Jackie had done wonders. After the Kennedys had been in office one year, Miss Beale wrote: "At every type of party the arrangements have been varied and impressive."

Jackie showed herself to be as creative a party giver as Mr. Onassis the night she arranged for the state dinner for the President of Pakistan, General Ayub Khan, to be held at Mount Vernon. Navy yachts were pressed into service to take the guests down the Potomac. Washroom facilities were somewhat primitive in General Washington's day, so Red Cross mobile units were pressed into service and parked on the lawn outside the mansion. After touring the historic home, the guests were served dinner outside under a perfect sky. The affair would have turned into a disaster if it had rained. When the possibility of rain was discussed at the White House, one staff member said: "The Lord wouldn't dare let it happen. Jackie would be fit to be tied."

Jackie herself has always favored sensitive French cooking over cruder American fare. One of the first things she did on entering the White House was to engage Master Chef René Verdon, who had been recommended by La Caravelle in New York. M. Verdon, in his starched white apron, tall chef's hat, and checked cotton pants, soon dominated, with Gallic intolerance, the staff of Filipino assistants who, during the Truman and Eisenhower administrations, had seldom been called on to produce anything more imaginative than roast beef and baked potatoes.

While President Kennedy usually enjoyed M. Verdon's *blanquette de veau*, he often longed for something more down to earth. But Jackie was determined, as she said, "not to run the White House as if it were a hash house." One night, when they were dining alone, Chef Verdon served them *quenelles Nantua*, a symphony of egg whites, pike, sole, and heavy cream crowned with lobster sauce. Yummy, but also gooey. Hardly the thing for a fellow's stomach, when he's spent half a frustrating day arguing with the Chairman of the House Appropriations Committee. Suddenly the President pushed his chair back and drummed his fork on the table. "For God's sake, Jackie," he exclaimed in vexation, "I am President of the most powerful nation on this earth, and I can get anything I want—*except* a simple hamburger."

As America's First Lady, Mrs. Kennedy had at her table some of the most eminent figures of contemporary history, and some of the most crashing bores. How many other women can say they discussed lions as house pets (in French) with Emperor Haile Selassie of Ethiopia? Or ribbed General Eisenhower, over a Scotch and soda, about his golf game? Or asked the wife of the Shah of Iran how to run a palace? Or discussed sailboating with Philip, Duke of Edinburgh.

Well, Mr. Onassis, without having any kind of official position, did pretty well on that score on his own long before he met Jackie. How many men can say they have hugged Elizabeth Taylor, as Ari did, at the French Lido, and other places; broken crockery in an Athenian *taverna* with Melina Mercouri; tipped an orchestra leader several hundred dollars to keep playing tangos to humor a whim of Maria Callas; and had, as his yacht guest for weeks at a time, Sir Winston Churchill?

Onassis' friendship with Sir Winston, when the giant of a man was nearing the end of the line, was a close and most touching association. Onassis kept Sir Winston jolly and active at a time when the old gentleman was usually surly and snappish. Lord Moran, who was Sir Winston's personal physician, recalled, in his diaries, one time when he and his famous patient were guests aboard the *Christina*.

"Winston has come to life," wrote Lord Moran. "Some of the credit must go to Ari. One moment he will fetch him a glass of whiskey, and the next he will tuck him in a blanket. Before dinner one night Ari pulled his chair nearer and held a teaspoonful of caviar to Winston's lips, as one feeds a baby."

If Onassis himself ever suffers bouts of temper or depression, he keeps the lid capped. Even when he has good cause for gloom he appears—superficially, at least— to be turned on. Some years back, one of his shipping combines made several unwise oil-cargo deals, and in a relatively short period *lost* $2,000,000. His assistants, as they discussed the calamity in Ari's Monte Carlo office, were depressed, self-critical, thoroughly defeated men.

"Oh, come now, this isn't a funeral!" said Ari, opening up his private bar, which is built into a wall and looks like a large safe. "I tell you what we'll do. Tomorrow we'll go out and *make* $2,000,000."

Onassis regards the evening as a time for play, and he will not tolerate any long faces around him. One time, in New York's El Morocco, he called over the late proprietor, John Perona, and said: "John, do me a favor. Get us another waiter. The fellow serving us now is competent, all right, but he's so bloody intense and serious you'd think he was serving the Last Supper."

Ari always seems so high that strangers often think he's out of his mind on booze, pills, or pot, which isn't so. One summer night he, Jackie, and his sister, Mrs. Garoufalidis, had dinner at a seaside *taverna* near the villa at Glyfada. As the evening wore on, and the *bouzouki* music got wilder and wilder, Ari and his sister, every ten minutes or so, sent a plate or cup crashing to the floor, out of simple exuberance. This is an ancient and honorable Greek custom—at least, it was. But these days the ruling junta has banned it as being "decadent." However, no one called in the police to haul Mr. Onassis off to the poky. Jackie, always as proper in public as Queen Elizabeth, was not amused by her husband's antics.

Ari's conduct that night recalled what Lucius Beebe had written, many years ago, about the cult customs of the powerful. The habit of the rich to smash things when they get stoned, said Mr. Beebe, set a pattern that closely followed the couplet to the effect that:

> *Like many of the upper class,*
> *He liked the sound of smashing glass.*

Mr. Onassis has the same capacity for stimulating beverages that he has for life—he takes them both in merry stride. At nightclubs there's always a bottle of Scotch by his elbow, and he'll take a sip, when the mood strikes him, but you'll never see him wobbly or running off silly at the mouth. The only time Ari feels he really "needs" a drink is at the end of a brutal business day, when million-dollar transcations have flown over the international telephone circuit like two-dollar bets at a race track. But in that Ari is no different from the thousands of American commuters who, on arriving home in their suburbs on the 5:26, rocket directly to the booze closet seeking a liquid nerve pacifier. The need to "unwind" is universal.

Three years ago, the Harvard School of Business Administration conducted a study of the interrelationship of alcohol consumption and executive success. "Those who worked more than sixty hours a week [par for Onassis] relax from the pressure by drink," said Harvard. "A 1967 survey of 391 members of the Princeton University class of 1942 showed that median income rose progressively with the number of drinks consumed."

Aristotle Onassis didn't happen to be a member of the Princeton class of '42, but it's unlikely he would contest the findings of the Harvard study. He seldom drinks to excess, but he likes to drink the deadly martini and insists that this liquid booby trap be as dry as the Sahara. One time, according to Willi Frischauer, one of his biographers, Mr. Onassis gave a dinner party for shipbuilding colleagues at Lambke's admirable restaurant in Hamburg. Lambke's staff is masterful when it comes to a good *Wiener schnitzel*, or a bottle of Alsatian wine, but the martini is as foreign to them as boiled missionary. When offered the yellowish liquid they had prepared, Ari made a face, slipped behind the bar, and mixed his own. They still talk about Onassis at Lambke's as "the richest bartender in the world."

Jackie has had to force herself to co-exist with her husband's dry martinis, for she feels that they should not be served by a bartender, but by an anesthetist. Not only that, but Jackie disapproves of her husband's pre-dinner smoking. Like anyone who cherishes superior cooking, Jackie believes that a man who has marinated his taste buds in tobacco and alcohol for thirty minutes couldn't tell the difference between a *foie gras* with truffles and a pizza.

It is a tribute to Jackie Onassis' willpower that, although she patronizes restaurants whose cookery is exquisitely rich, she can still get into her debutante-ball gown without using a shoehorn. Today she is smaller than in many years—down to a size six. While she does not necessarily approve of shoplifting, arson, forgery, or genocide, as far as she is concerned the only real crime is *fat*. So, wherever she is, she eats very sparingly, nibbling at the most succulent dishes like a dyspeptic sparrow; half a cracker with caviar, a few mouthfuls of the roast, one spoonful of the ice cream. Jackie is like all girls of the international set; each in her own miserable way is starving in the midst of plenty. Jackie's close friend "Bunny" Mellon summed up the problem when she said: "No girl can be too rich—or too thin."

(One of the Pinkerton detectives who guard Jackie in New York does not possess her talent for sparse eating. Wherever she lunches or dines, he also takes his meals, at another table or in the kitchen. Last year he put on twenty pounds, and had to go on an enervating Metrecal-and-cottage-cheese diet.)

For breakfast, which she regularly takes in bed, Jackie has orange juice, toast, and honey. She uses skimmed milk and artificial sweeteners with her tea and coffee. If, for some incomprehensible reason, she stays home all day—perhaps the area is paralyzed by a general strike—her lunch and dinner will be hardly more than an omelette or ground meat and salad. One of her few caloric indulgences is a nightcap before she goes to bed, but usually nothing stronger than a single daiquiri. She likes them made with two parts rum, three parts frozen limeade, one part fresh lime juice, and a few drops of artificial sweetener.

From time to time Jackie takes, to reduce her appetite,

a "diet" pill. She also drops in, every once in a while, to talk about the preservation of her figure, which is something worth talking about, with Dr. Jerome Klein, the New York physician who has taken off inches and inches from fashionable abdomens and thighs whose owners are listed in the Social Register, Burke's Peerage, Dun and Bradstreet's, and with Actors' Equity.

Right up to the time she married Mr. Onassis, Jackie attended, usually once a week, the New York gymnastic studio of the internationally famous exercise teacher Nicholas Kounovsky. Mr. Kounovsky gave Jackie a program of jerks and pulls and stretches and bends that, he says, "is aimed to exercise every muscle in the body." She does the Kounovsky exercises every midmorning.

There was a rumor that Jackie had taken up yoga. It began to circulate the morning a socialite, on the deck of her yacht in Nassau, was peeping, through powerful binoculars, at Jackie, who was on deck of the *Christina*, which was anchored nearby. When observed by the peeper, Jackie, wearing a leotard, was on her back and her legs were jackknifed over her head. The spying lady immediately reported to anyone who would listen—and many did—that she had seen Jackie, "with my own eyes," performing a spiritual ritual of the ancient East. The same lady also reported that she had seen, through her long glasses, Mr. Onassis slumped in a deck chair a few feet from his energetic wife, reading the *Wall Street Journal*.

This nonsense about Jackie and yoga wound up in the newspapers, and Jackie had yet another score to settle with the press.

Standing on her head is one of the more restful activities Jackie Onassis participated in during the first year of her marriage, and thereafter for that matter. It is difficult to comprehend how peripatetic jet setters of this top drawer category really are without accompanying them on their restless travels.

Since that would be slightly difficult to arrange, let's do the next best thing and chart the comings and goings of Jackie and Ari, in tandem and solo, for a solid year. It breaks down as follows for the first year of their marriage.

KEEPING UP WITH THE ONASSISES

A month-by-month chronicle of Jackie and Ari's travels during their first year of marriage

OCTOBER
October 20, 1968, America's former First Lady married to billionaire Aristotle Socrates Onassis in Greek Orthodox chapel on Skorpios Island in the Ionian Sea.
After one day on the island, Caroline and John Kennedy fly back to New York.
Immediately after wedding Ari starts commuting to Athens, where he's trying to make $400,000,000 deal with the ruling military junta. He stays away several nights.
Vatican says Jackie now cut off from sacraments for knowingly marrying a divorced man.
Jackie sightsees alone on nearby islands, riding a donkey.

NOVEMBER
Eleven days after the wedding, Jackie and Ari start a short delayed honeymoon, cruising on the *Christina*.
Jackie flies to London.
Ari flies to Paris, meets with Maria Callas, supposedly to "explain" marriage.
Ari joins Jackie at Lee Radziwill's home, Turville Heath, England. While they're there $12,000 in jewels stolen from estate.
Jackie flies to New York, marks fifth anniversary of

President Kennedy's assassination in seclusion with her children.

Ari flies from London to Paris, gives swinging party at Regine's in Montparnasse.

Jackie rides to hounds with Essex Hunt, near Peapack, N.J.

Jackie flies to Washington, visits graves of President Kennedy and Senator Robert Kennedy.

Ari flies to New York, first night there dines at "21" with his daughter, Christina, and with his sister.

Ari flies to Paris, then on to Skorpios.

DECEMBER
Ari flies to New York, gives party at El Morocco for friends and relatives; Jackie absent.

Fashion magazine writes: "New Yorkers are buzzing about the fact that *the* newlyweds never seem to go out together."

Ari buys Jackie sable coat on Fifth Avenue.

Ari returns to Europe, buys ten ringside seats for Benvenuti-Fullmer fight in San Remo, Italy.

The departure of Jackie and her children for Athens delayed four hours while police search for bomb on her plane at Kennedy Airport and find nothing.

Jackie, Ari, and the children celebrate Christmas on the *Christina.*

JANUARY, 1969
Jackie and children return to New York without Ari.

Jackie buys "priceless" *objets d'art* at A La Vieille Russie.

Ari reported on secret trip to Yokohama drydocks.

Ari flies to New York. He and Jackie entertain at La Côte Basque. Check is $927.

Ari flies to Paris, entertains eleven at Maxim's.

Jackie weekends at Hyannis Port.

Ari flies to Skorpios.

FEBRUARY
Jackie flies to Switzerland, visits sister Lee, who is in sanatorium.

Ari flies from Skorpios to Paris, makes the nightclubs with actress Elsa Martinelli.

Jackie flies back to New York, attends theater with young architect Edward Barnes.

Jackie lunches with Doris Duke, then hides in a hallway for an hour, dodging photographers.

Ari flies to New York.

Jackie and Ari fly to Palm Beach, visit ailing Joseph P. Kennedy in his villa.

Jackie and Ari, back in New York, create sensation at P. J. Clarke's Third Avenue saloon when curious women follow Jackie into powder room.

MARCH

Ari flies to Rome, confers with exiled Greek King Constantine and his mother, Queen Frederika, an old intimate friend.

Jackie makes the rounds of the smart new East Side bistros with, as one paper puts it, "bachelors and borrowed husbands."

Jackie flies to Paris for a few days, then flies to Switzerland to visit Lee.

Jackie flies from Geneva to Las Palmas in the Canary Islands.

Ari steams into Las Palmas aboard the *Christina*.

APRIL

Jackie and Ari make an eight-day cruise across the Atlantic, winding up in Trinidad.

The *Christina* drops anchor in Nassau. There Jackie and Ari seen at Greek Orthodox church, holding candles at midnight mass and kissing three times, according to ancient Orthodox custom.

Jackie and Ari fly to New York. Ari gets estimates on building a town house at 71st Street and Park Avenue. Ari makes six-day trip to Paris.

Jackie and Ari fly to Palm Beach to rejoin the *Christina*, but yacht too large for local marina, must dock in less fashionable Miami.

Christina steams to Nassau, where Rose Kennedy is welcomed aboard with Caroline and John.

MAY
Ari flies to Paris, London, Athens.
Jackie goes on wildest shopping spree of her career in New York, spending thousands every day. Trade paper calls her "the retailer's best friend."
At a party in New York, Truman Capote's dog chews up Lee Radziwill's sable coat. Prince Radziwill is furious, Jackie amused.
Jackie takes Caroline and John on a picnic in Central Park. A Secret Serviceman carries the basket.
Ari flies to New York.
Jackie and the children attend mass to mark what would have been John Fitzgerald Kennedy's fifty-second birthday.

JUNE
Ari disappears from New York, said to be competing with Howard Hughes in Las Vegas, buying hotels and gambling casinos.
Ari flies alone to Paris, runs into Maria Callas at a party. She gives him hell in four languages—English, French, Italian, and Greek. Ari laughs it off, next day sends her a small diamond.
Jackie flies to Paris.
Jackie and Ari fly to Nice, pick up the *Christina* at Monte Carlo.
Ari and Jackie cruise to Skorpios, stopping at Villefranche, San Remo, and Capri en route.

JULY
Caroline and John Kennedy fly to Skorpios for a holiday.
Greek police investigate wild plot to kidnap Jackie. Junta censors all mention of incident.
On July 28th, Jackie's fortieth birthday, Ari gives her over $1,000,000 in jewels, including a diamond as big as the Ritz.

Jackie starts redecorating villa at Glyfada.
Ari flies to Paris.

AUGUST

Jackie and children, without Ari, make an extended tour
of ancient Greek shrines, including Mt. Olympus.
Ari flies from Paris to Hamburg to inspect shipyard con-
structing one of his tankers.
Ari flies to Skorpios the day that the Athens office of
Olympic Airlines—an Onassis property—is bombed. Police blame "anti-junta elements." Anti-junta pamphlet
accuses Ari of being "banker" for the junta.
Jackie flies alone to Rome to see Antonio's fall models,
buys heavily.
Jackie and Ari meet in Paris. Parisian daily reports:
"They are in and out of their Avenue Foch apartment
at all hours—the Rolls-Royces keep coming and going—
but they never leave together."

SEPTEMBER

Jackie flies alone to New York.
Parisian designer Coco Chanel blasts Jackie. Says
Coco: "She has horrible taste. She tries to look like her
own little daughter by wearing little girl clothes."
Jackie, cycling in Central Park with Caroline and John,
has pursuing photographer arrested.
Ari flies to New York.
Jackie and Ari are on the town every night, spending
some evenings well over $1,000 for themselves and their
guests in such night spots as Raffles.
London paper reports Ari now worth over one *billion*.

OCTOBER

Jackie allegedly uses judo to flip photographer who bugs
her as she leaves the movie *I Am Curious (Yellow)*.
Ari flies to Washington on hush-hush business.
Jackie lunches with Ethel Kennedy, first time in many
months.
On October 20th, their first anniversary, Ari gives Jackie

another $1,000,000 in jewels at a party in their Fifth Avenue apartment. Guests are stunned.

During the first year of marriage, Jackie and Ari have been together 225 days, apart 140 days.

Chapter Fourteen

JACKIE
VS. THE PRESS

On the afternoon of October 6, 1969, the city desks of New York newspapers and national news agencies were advised, over the telephone, by the publicity-seeking manager of Cinema Rendezvous, on West 57th Street, that Mr. and Mrs. Aristotle Onassis were attending a performance, in his movie theater, of the sexually "liberated" Swedish film *I am Curious (Yellow)*.

Such is the news value of the Onassises that minutes after the theater manager called, a large number of cameramen converged on the theater, taking up strategic points both inside and out. Mr. Melvin Finkelstein, of the New York *Daily News*, was on duty on the sidewalk in front of Cinema Rendezvous when Jackie—alone— emerged. (Jackie, who is something of a Victorian, left the movie before it was over. Ari, who isn't, stayed to the

end—so he missed the fracas that took place on the sidewalk outside the theater.)

According to Mr. Finkelstein, Mrs. Onassis (who was
sick and tired of constantly being hounded by the press)
"came toward me from my right, grabbed my right arm,
put her left leg out, and flipped me right over it."

Mr. Finkelstein had nothing but admiration for what he
described as Jackie's excellent employment of judo. He
said that in the pursuit of his profession, which many people find irritating, "I've been flipped by the best, including
Frank Sinatra's bodyguards. But Jackie's flip was the
fastest and smoothest job I ever had to suffer."

The next day Mrs. Onassis, about 120 pounds, issued a
statement in which she denied laying a glove on the 168-
pound photographer. And an eyewitness said he saw Mr.
Finkelstein trip over himself, which is a neat trick. The
following week *Variety*, the weekly show-business journal,
reported that the Onassises' publicized visit to Cinema
Rendezvous was worth $21,527 to the house. "This week's
gross," said *Variety*, "was $34,415 as against the pre-
Jackie Onassis week when the take was $12,843."

Whatever the facts concerning Mr. Finkelstein's abrupt
descent to the pavement in front of the fortunate picture
house are, the incident was just another chapter in the
perpetual struggle between Jackie and the photographic
corps, a struggle that is now ten years old. The first shot
was fired early in 1960 when the then Senator John
Kennedy gained national prominence by campaigning for
the Democratic Presidential nomination. One afternoon
Mrs. Kennedy was quietly sitting under the drier in a
Washington beauty parlor when she was distracted by
sounds of screeching and shoving. A pushing-and-swearing
match was in progress between two hairdressers and a

photographer the hairdressers had intercepted as he tried to infiltrate the salon with the intention of taking some candid shots of Jackie. Ever since then, as America's First Lady, then as Mrs. Onassis, Jackie has been trying to avoid the candid camera.

Dining with friends in Maxim's in Paris, Jackie discussed the photographers who were always pursuing her. She is reported to have said: "They seem to be everywhere. I would not be surprised to have a flashbulb go off in my face when I'm in the shower."

While such an invasion is yet to be recorded, it certainly is not because the photographers do not try. One time, when she was staying in New York's Carlyle Hotel, a photographer tried to enter her suite disguised as a room-service waiter. Three years ago, when Mrs. Kennedy was swimming off Waikiki on a Hawaiian holiday, an athletic photographer followed her on a surfboard with a water-proof camera.

It is not only the photographers employed by recognized news media who are always tailing Jackie. A regiment of free-lancers are also on hand simply because a good set of pictures of Mrs. Onassis, sold throughout the world, can earn a year's income. (Sneak shots of Ari and Jackie kissing on the deck of the *Christina*, taken with a tele-scopic lens, have already brought over $50,000, and they're still selling. The New York *Daily News* paid $1,200 for one shot from the set for a single printing.)

Probably the most persistent photographic free-lancer bugging Jackie is a man named Ron Galella, who operates on two continents, an international *paparazzo*. One night last winter Galella was tipped off, by the proprietor of a restaurant in New York's Chinatown, that Mr. and Mrs. Onassis had just sat down, with some friends, to a dinner that included shark's-fin soup. Galella hurried downtown from his Bronx basement studio, slipped into the establishment, and concealed himself in a coat rack with a good view of the eminent couple. At his whispered request, the proprietor turned up the volume on the radio so that Galella's subject, only a few feet away, wouldn't hear the clicking of his Nikon.

Besides merchants and restaurateurs anxious for public identity with the Onassises, Galella is aided by volunteer, unpaid Jackie-watchers. He circulates among the incurable rubberneckers whose hobby is hanging around outside Jackie's New York apartment, distributes his card, and says: "Give me a holler whenever she leaves the house."

One afternoon last October, one of these gapers rushed to a telephone to report to Galella that Mrs. Onassis, her son John, and three bodyguards had gone bicycling in the park. Galella, his camera in a duffle bag slung over his shoulder, raced downtown to the park, and quickly found the Kennedys and escort cycling along a path in convoy. He whipped out his Nikon and ran alongside Jackie and John, Jr., clicking away.

Mrs. Onassis sighed: "Oh, it's you again." She smiled into the camera, but through her teeth she said to a bodyguard: "Mr. Connelly, smash his camera."

Mr. Connelly did no such thing, but the police did arrest Galella on a charge of harassment. (The case was later thrown out of court.)

For his thirty minutes in the park, Galella said he would make $2,000 out of the pictures, including $800 from the Associated Press, which prides itself on its dignity. Discussing his career as a Jackie-watcher, he told a reporter: "You have to be part detective and part actor. I even went as far as to date one of Mr. Onassis' maids. Jackie is the most difficult of all celebrities to photograph. Liz Taylor won't run away when she sees me, but Jackie will. And so sometimes I wear my sunglasses or my hippie wig so as not to be recognized. It's sort of a game I play."

One time, when Mr. and Mrs. Onassis emerged from a restaurant, there, as usual, was Galella. Mr. Onassis shook his head and asked: "Isn't there an easier way to make a living? Why, you look at us as if we were targets."

One of the boldest attempts to invade Jackie's privacy took place when she visited Greece, in the summer of 1961, after accompanying the President to Vienna for a conference with Soviet leader Nikita Khrushchev. Marcos Nomikos, one of the richest of the Greek shipping men, put his yacht at the First Lady's disposal, and she made a slow tour of the Aegean Islands. The Greek government had provided a police launch to keep photographers, in their chartered boats, a good distance from the Nomikos yacht. Later, Letitia Baldridge, who was in Greece with Mrs. Kennedy as her social and press secretary, said: "The Greek police and our Secret Service managed to keep the press away from her by land and by sea—including an attack on her yacht by camera-armed frogmen who appeared from the depths of the Aegean."

Ironically, the only job Mrs. Onassis ever held (after graduating from Miss Porter's School in Farmington, Connecticut, and studying at Vassar, the University of Grenoble, and the Sorbonne) was as a *photographer* for the old Washington *Times Herald*. When her stint as a photographer is mentioned, Jackie's defenders hasten to point out that she didn't go around sneaking up on people like a cat burglar. Miss Bouvier was employed as an "inquiring photographer." That is, with a camera of those days, something the size of a shoe box, she was assigned to stop passersby in the streets, snap their pictures, record their names and addresses, then ask such penetrating questions, prepared in advance by the feature desk, as "What do you think of teen-age marriage?" Or: "Does your husband smoke in bed?"

Jacqueline Bouvier regarded the whole business as something of a lark; she was often accompanied by chums who tittered in the background as she struggled to manipulate the camera, as alien to her as a pneumatic drill. One citizen, photographed in front of the Washington Monument, wrote to the editor of the *Times Herald:* "A young lady from your paper took my picture and, giggling all the while, asked me if my wife expected me to shave before breakfast. I wonder if she was actually in your employ or, which is more likely, was she being initiated into a sorority?"

Frankly, Jackie's photographs will never be immortalized along with those of Matthew Brady or Edward Steichen—or, for that matter, those of Melvin Finkelstein. One day she was summoned to the photo department and told that her pictures were too often out of focus. It was suggested that she always stand six feet from her subject. Jackie, in her breathless voice, said: "But how can I tell how far is six feet?" One of the photographers stretched himself on his back on the floor, his toes to Jackie's toes, and said: "Now, see my head? That's approximately six feet from you."

Jackie's career as a photographer lasted only slightly more than a year; she retired with her marriage to the then Senator John F. Kennedy.

Those who knew her during the White House years say Jackie was well aware that the wife of a President facing re-election shouldn't be rude to a legitimate photographer. But she did practice a certain amount of deception, and she became an expert at sneaking in and out of places without being photographed.

When the President urged his wife not to dress flamboyantly, or in any way display great wealth, Jackie tried to oblige. For instance, she never wore her favorite double-breasted mink coat when there was a chance that photographers would be covering her. However, after the President was killed and she moved to New York, one fashion reporter wrote: "Her double-breasted black mink coat from Maximilian's has become one of her uniforms for afternoon errands."

In the White House or out, Jackie has won one skirmish with the photographers—the Battle of the Cigarettes. Jackie does smoke—moderately—but she has some pretty conservative, if somewhat old-fashioned ideas, on a lady's proper deportment, and one of them is that a lady should never be photographed while smoking. When she has a cigarette, Jackie keeps one eye peeled for roving photographers. There are only a few pictures of Jackie with a cigarette.

Jackie won a complete victory over the photographers —and just about everybody else, for that matter—during the time she was being courted by Aristotle Onassis. To hide their romance, Aristotle Onassis and Jacqueline Kennedy used methods of camouflage and deception worthy of *Mission Impossible*. In the summer of 1967 Mr. Onassis would leave his suite in the Hotel Pierre, announcing that he'd be "out of town" for a few days, then drive, in his chauffered limousine, to Times Square. There he would wait for Mrs. Kennedy, who would arrive in a taxi from her Fifth Avenue apartment. Then they'd go, in Mr. Onassis' car, to the ranch house Jackie had rented in Peapack, New Jersey. The photographers really missed the bus on that one. Although Mr. Onassis became a familiar figure, strolling around Peapack, not one camera recorded his presence.

Jackie's struggle for freedom from photographers has been a losing proposition since the day she married Mr. Onassis. Even the wedding itself was marred by an unsightly brawl between photographers from just about every country in the world and Mr. Onassis' employees on Skorpios. The day of the wedding, the fight to get to the island began when flotillas of small boats, carrying reporters and photographers, clashed with sailors from the *Christina* and Onassis' special guards. One observer wrote: "Onassis had begged Jackie to permit a planeload of selected journalists to cover the wedding in order to avoid the disgraceful fracas that surrounded the ceremony, but her hostility to the press had been strengthened when, on the eve of her wedding, her seven-year-old son had been approached and asked what he thought of his mother's wedding."

Since the Battle of the Wedding, Jackie's temper, which is likely to blow at the best of times, seems to explode at the mere sight of an uninvited camera, as it allegedly did in New York, outside the theater showing *I Am Curious (Yellow)*.

Is all this a put-on? Over and over again, Mr. and Mrs. Onassis have said they are entitled to live their own lives, like everybody else, without having reporters and photographers in their hair. But their professed desire for privacy is often contradicted by the way they conduct themselves. If the Onassises were really shattered every time they were made a fuss of in public—while cameras snapped—

it would be easy for them, with all their resources, to live well off the urban mainstream as absolute recluses. Actually, the way Jackie and Ari live seems almost to *solicit* publicity.

Privacy-seeking New Yorkers, whose faces are as well known as Jackie's and Ari's, do not, as the Onassises do, dine at "21" or Trader Vic's or Le Pavillon. There are hundreds of quite decent eating places in Manhattan that have never become goldfish bowls. Nor do privacy seekers, as the Onassises claim to be, exchange friendly chitchat with gossip columnists. Last October, columnist Leonard Lyons wrote that he had been at La Côte Basque, and that Mr. Onassis had invited him to sit down at their table and have a drink with them—hardly the gesture of a man defending his privacy.

Some of Jackie's friends say she has a "love-hate" complex about the press—she really can't make up her mind. Perhaps she recalls what Oscar Wilde wrote, in *The Picture of Dorian Gray:* "There is only one thing in the world worse than being talked about, and that is not being talked about."

Probably what Mr. Onassis is trying to do, when he makes a friendly overture to Leonard Lyons, is to create a situation that might someday lead to an armed truce between him and his wife and the gentlemen of the press. Perhaps he envisages a peace conference, with himself on one side of the table and a representative of the world's journalists on the other. But he knows he can't permanently shake the photographers. "The worst thing that can happen to a man," he has said, "is to become a celebrity. It's as though there was a law that you have to walk naked in public—no matter how well you are, they make you look ridiculous."

In fairness to the highly competitive photographers, who, many citizens think, have been giving Jackie a hard time, it should be said that not only photographers are curious about her. One night last winter Mr. and Mrs. Onassis dropped into P. J. Clarke's, a kind of jet-set saloon on New York's Third Avenue, for some cheeseburgers and steins of beer. All eyes were on them from the moment they entered. When Mrs. Onassis left the table and went to the powder room, at least eight ordinarily well-mannered women followed her. Jackie, after elbowing her way out of the overcrowded place, stomped back to her table mumbling angrily. The owner, Mr. Dan Lavazzo, apologetic about the embarrassing event, assured Mr. Onassis that if he and his wife would be kind enough to patronize the establishment again, a special guard would be posted before the powder room to control traffic.

PART FIVE

Good-Bye, Hyannis Port

Chapter Fifteen

JACKIE AND
THE KENNEDYS

One doesn't have to tap a single Kennedy telephone to know that Jackie Onassis has drifted quite apart from the Hyannis Port family circle. The split began when the Kennedys opposed her marriage to Aristotle Onassis. Then, when Joseph P. Kennedy died—and he was a colossus in Jackie's eyes—the last emotional link was gone. If it were not for the children, John and Caroline, the split, by this time, would probably be complete.

Jackie and Ethel or Joan will still have a difficult frigid lunch once in a while, and Rose Kennedy will visit the *Christina* for a day or two in Greece, or during the Palm Beach season, when the yacht cruises off Florida. But friendship, a warm family relationship—that doesn't really exist any more.

The truth of the matter is that neither Jackie nor her

sister, Lee, was ever really at home with the Kennedys, except for the former Ambassador, old Joe Kennedy, and, to a lesser extent, the ever-gracious Rose. Jackie and Lee simply could not tolerate the "Kennedy atmosphere," always political, and they disliked and made fun of the "Irish Mafia." Jackie herself confided to friends that the long visits to the Kennedy homes at Palm Beach and Hyannis Port were unpleasant experiences. One observer said that Hyannis Port, for Jackie, became a place of strange men on the telephone, strange men in the rooms, press men outside the house, barely a few feet away, and press conferences at Bobby's house. She never knew whom she would meet at the breakfast table, nor who would still be there for a last drink at night.

At the dinner table, when all the members of the clan dined together, the conversation invariably turned to politics, and it was often loud and argumentative. Jackie was raised in a gentler atmosphere. Voices were never raised, and religion and politics were two subjects that were never discussed at dinner.

People near Jackie, when she was the First Lady, often sensed the underlying tension between her and the other Kennedy women, particularly Ethel. Ethel was quite content to be the usually-pregnant busy wife of a busy politician. The way Jackie saw it, Ethel's home in Hickory Hill was as middle-class as Grand Rapids—overstuffed sofas and, everywhere you looked, television sets blaring away, cowboys chasing Indians, Red Skelton, Huntley and Brinkley.

Jackie preferred giving dinner parties with the whitest tablecloths, and candles burning, and heavy silver, and the finest French fare. Ethel preferred to entertain at barbecues. The story is told that one day, at a family outing aboard the Kennedy yacht *Honeyfitz*, when lunchtime came, the Kennedy clan, dressed in comfortable old blue jeans, sprawled on the foredeck eating sandwiches and drinking beer out of cans. Meanwhile, Jackie and Lee, impeccably attired in the proper yachting costumes featured in the fashion magazines, were served chilled crab and white wine on the fantail by a steward in a white coat.

With the possible exception of Pat Lawford, Jackie has never been close to the women of the Kennedy clan—not Ted's wife, Joan, and certainly not Ethel, with all that running downfield to catch a pass, and all those noisy kids underfoot all the time. They just aren't Jackie's cup of tea.

She was not very comfortable with Bobby, either. He just couldn't seem to relax, and when he did it was usually to play crude practical jokes, like pushing people who were fully dressed into his swimming pool, which she disapproved of. A lot of people in the capital felt the same way, and it was suggested that when Bobby sent out invitations for a formal dinner, they should read: "Black tie and snorkel."

But when his brother was shot, Jackie found Bobby her most understanding friend. She said: "He's the one I'd put my hand in the fire for." But she "lost" Bobby when she became engaged to Aristotle Onassis.

Jackie's attitude toward Joseph P. Kennedy was something else. In fact, his death last November was a terrible blow to her. Some years ago, when she was married to John Kennedy, she told her intimates, and even told several reporters, that "next to my husband and my own father, I love Joe Kennedy more than anybody in the world."

To understand Jackie's fascination with the senior Kennedy, one must remember how close Jackie was to her own father, John Vernon Bouvier. When John Bouvier died, in 1952, Jackie began to admire, then to love and depend on Joseph Kennedy. Joseph Kennedy, in a way, replaced her own father. Mary Barelli Gallagher, Mrs. Kennedy's private secretary during the White House years, discussing Joseph Kennedy, said: "What I remember most, when I think of Mr. Kennedy, is the great fondness Jackie held for him. They could sit and happily scheme together and be as playful as two little children."

Jackie's love for Joseph Kennedy was far from instantaneous, and in this she was somewhat influenced by her own father. John Bouvier always became furious when anyone so much as mentioned Joseph Kennedy by name, and he almost had a fit when Jackie decided to marry one of Joseph Kennedy's sons. A man who had been associated with John Bouvier told this writer, not long ago: "John Bouvier reacted to the news that his daughter was going to marry Joe Kennedy's son the way Barry Goldwater would react to the news that his daughter was going to marry a son of Mao Tse-Tung."

The reason Joseph Kennedy always set Mr. Bouvier off like a booby trap is that Franklin Roosevelt, early in his administration, had appointed Joseph Kennedy head of the Securities and Exchange Commission and Kennedy ruthlessly tightened up many loose practices. John Bouvier, who was very active as a Wall Street trader, had a series of bitter battles with the SEC. According to John Davies, one of Jackie's cousins, who wrote a book about the family, "John Bouvier felt that Joe Kennedy had played the market for all it was worth—then he proceeded to end all the practices he had made his money from."

Naturally, Jackie approached her father-in-law with caution. And from the beginning she bristled under the senior Kennedy's autocratic rule of the clan of which, it was assumed, she had automatically become a loyal, servile member. One time Jackie told an old friend from Vassar: "The Ambassador [as she always referred to Joseph Kennedy] acts like he's a general and all the rest of the family, including his in-laws, are privates; there are no ranks in between."

Jackie, always somewhat of a loner and independent as a cat, did not favor the Kennedy custom of doing everything *en masse*. During one long weekend at Hyannis Port, for example, Kennedy Senior had arranged a program in practically a military "Order of the Day" manner. At a certain hour all the Kennedys, their wives and their children were to climb into cars and be driven to church. Then, at another hour, everybody was expected to sit around and read the newspapers, which were flown in from many cities. Then it would be time for a game of touch football; Kennedy Senior said who was to be on what side, and, of course, he was the referee. Jackie did not like touch football; in fact, she never quite understood the game. (Theodore Sorenson, often a Hyannis Port guest, recalls that in one huddle "Jackie said to me: 'Just tell me, when I get the ball which way do I run?'")

All the many, many Kennedys dined together at a huge table, and old Joe was at the head, and the food was passed around amid a bedlam that reminded some visitors of the court of Henry VIII. Old Joe, of course, *was* Henry, and when everyone had had his fill, he would clear his throat and toss a topic for conversation in the air and let the others grab it. "Old Joe presided at the dinner table as if it were a meeting of the board of directors and he was the chairman," said one onlooker.

The dinners proved exhausting for Jackie, and very often she claimed a headache and was served dinner on a tray in her room.

Things came to a head one time when the President and Jackie were staying at Joseph Kennedy's palm Beach home and she arrived fifteen minutes late for lunch. A family friend who was present recalls what happened then: "That sort of tardiness could be fatal with the Ambassador when he was in one of his Emperor Augustus moods. So when Jackie came in he started to give her the needle—and she gave it right back. Old Joe had a lot of old-fashioned slang phrases, so Jackie told him: "You ought to write a series of grandfather stories for children, like 'The Duck with Moxie,' and 'The Donkey Who Couldn't Fight His Way Out of a Telephone Booth.'"

Everybody was stunned by Jackie's sarcastic rebellion. It was as if someone had laughed in church. There wasn't a sound. Then Kennedy Senior, realizing how ridiculous the situation had become, laughed out loud.

From that point on, he showed respect for Jackie's life style, for her determination to go her own way. He took pains to treat her as an individual, not as just another private in the ranks. He used his considerable charm to get to know her better, to win her friendship, and, like almost everything he did in life, he was immensely successful. In public he almost seemed to be encouraging Jackie to spar with him. Richard J. Whalen, in his biography of Joseph Kennedy, wrote that Jackie painted a watercolor for her father-in-law. It showed a crowd of young Kennedys on the beach, looking out to sea. "You can't take it with you," read the caption. "Dad's got it all."

Jackie never hesitated to defy the senior Kennedy if she felt he was being highhanded. One time, Joe Kennedy gathered the clan to celebrate the then Senator John Kennedy's birthday in New York's Le Pavillon. Anxious to preserve the moment, the senior Kennedy phoned for a photographer to come over.

Joseph Kennedy had overlooked Henri Soule, Le Pavillon's proprietor and himself an absolute autocrat. M. Soule had a firm rule—no photographers. When M. Soule saw the cameraman arrive with elaborate equipment, he acted as if a camel caravan wanted to use the washroom. He blocked the entrance and held his position firm, despite Joseph Kennedy's frantic appeals.

Such a thing could not be endured, and Joseph Kennedy announced to the clan that Le Pavillon was now off limits. And so it was to all of them—except Jackie, who showed up for lunch a few days later.

Jackie enjoyed putting down the senior Kennedy, from time to time, in good spirits. For years he had been fond of repeating that he had given each one of his children $1,000,000 when they had reached their maturity.

"I did this," he would say, "so they could be independent, and, if they wished, could tell me to go to hell."

When Mr. Kennedy told his story to Jackie, she asked him: "Do you know what I would tell you if you gave me $1,000,000?"

"No."

"I would tell you to give me another $1,000,000."

On another occasion, shortly before the Democratic primaries in 1960, a wild rumor spread around New York

to the effect that Senator Kennedy and Jackie had had a
severe falling out, and that Joseph Kennedy had offered
Jackie $1,000,000 not to divorce her husband until after
the election.

When Jackie heard the rumor she telephoned the
Ambassador and snapped: "Cheapskate!"

Joe Kennedy, in turn, enjoyed ribbing Jackie. Particularly about her weakness for buying clothes. In 1960,
Women's Wear Daily created something of a sensation
when it reported that Jackie and her mother-in-law, Rose
Kennedy, had between them spent $30,000 on a shopping
spree in Paris. When the women returned to the United
States and Hyannis Port, Kennedy made quite a thing
about it, and insisted that they show him—and all assembled—"exactly what I got for my money."

Jackie and Rose took it all in stride and obliged. They
paraded their latest acquisitions before the entire clan
while Joseph Kennedy acted as the master of ceremonies,
although he couldn't tell a Balenciaga from a Dior.

A few years ago Jackie told a writer that she was more
like Joseph Kennedy than anyone else in his family, including his own children. Indeed, as a certain secret
chemistry brought them ever closer together, Jackie
seemed to arouse in the Ambassador a sense of humor
and youthful zest that the rest of his kinfolk left dormant.
Bobby, for example, was, as Jackie so often said, "So
God-awful serious." And the other Kennedy wives, Ethel
and Joan, well, they never sparkled like Jackie, they never
set the old man's eyes dancing as she did. They really
had a thing between them, Jackie and old Joe Kennedy.
Sometimes Jackie and the Ambassador cut up delicious
little touches together that mystified, and often appalled,

the others. One such caper took place in the dining room of the house in Palm Beach during Christmas of 1960.

Evelyn Jones, the long-time Kennedy housekeeper, was passing through the dining room during the main course when Jackie and the Ambassador made a bet. The winner would be the one who could first hit Evelyn Jones with a lamb chop before she could get to the pantry door.

In the years before Joseph Kennedy had his stroke, Jackie brought to him any problems that she regarded as serious. From persons who were on John Kennedy's staff, when he was a Senator, and later, when he was the Chief Executive, I learned that these "serious" problems invariably concerned Jackie's inability, and often downright unwillingness, to do all the things expected of the wife of an ambitious public figure.

Evelyn Lincoln, who was President Kennedy's personal secretary, Letitia Baldridge, who was Jackie's social secretary, Ted Sorenson, and Mrs. Gallagher all agreed that Jackie simply did not have the interest or the drive to undertake the many obligations normally assigned to a First Lady. She didn't deny her distaste for the political limelight. "It is not my cup of tea," she told the senior Kennedy.

Joseph Kennedy took the good-natured attitude that no one really expected Jackie to be like Eleanor Roosevelt, and visit a coal mine or inspect an electrical power project. The Ambassador said: "Let's face it, Jackie. You haven't got the proper clothes for that kind of stuff."

But, under his direction, she did make some concessions to her husband's desire for her to play a large role. She visited children's hospitals and allowed herself to become honorary president of a number of charitable drives and institutions.

The President also sought his father's counsel when Jackie was "kicking up a storm." He asked the Ambassador, on one occasion, to try to get Jackie to modify her headline-catching wardrobe, which had been seized on by the opposition for some rather heavyhanded funmaking. During this period Joseph Kennedy remarked to an old friend: "I spent a good part of my life putting women into the best clothes money can buy. Now I'm trying to get one out of them."

One thing was clear—the Ambassador was just about the only man who could get Jackie to cool it when her back was up.

The Kennedy boys' total dedication to the pursuit of their careers often depressed Jackie. This was particularly so in 1960, when John F. Kennedy made his successful bid for the Presidency. During the entire campaign, to Jackie's amazement, Joseph Kennedy was, for all practical purposes, kept out of sight. This because the old gentleman was regarded, politically, as Arthur Schlesinger, Jr., said quite frankly, as "a hot potato." The senior Kennedy had incurred the wrath of a fair percentage of the older generation by taking, in the days immediately preceding World War II, what was regarded as an isolationist view.

One of the major news magazines had a story to the effect that Jack was running for President, Bobby was managing the campaign, and Ted was in charge of hiding Joseph P. Kennedy. The Ambassador spent a good part of the period in a villa he had rented for the summer on the French Riviera. He returned in time to vote, and when he appeared in Washington for the Inaugural Ball he walked over to Jackie, put his arm around her, and said: "Well, tonight's the payoff."

However, this hide-and-seek game, during the campaign, had left a deep and unfavorable impression on Jackie—one, according to her close friends, that she was never to forget. Often she blurted right out, to the consternation of the Kennedy brothers, that "even the Presidency of the United States is not worth having if you have to hide your own father to obtain it." The shenanigans which so distressed Jackie were repeated, to some extent, in May of 1968 when Jackie told the Kennedy clan she intended to marry Aristotle Onassis. Since Bobby was then engaged in his primary fight for the Democratic Presidential nomination, and Mr. Onassis' reputation was hardly a vote getter, Jackie had to be persuaded to keep her plans a secret until the nomination was decided. She told her intimates that she did so, because "I know this is what the Ambassador would want me to do."

Cardinal Cushing, who later defended Jackie's right to marry Mr. Onassis, has said he is sure that if Joseph Kennedy had had control of all his faculties at the time, he too would have given Jackie and Ari his blessing.

One of the most ironic notes in the Kennedy saga is Joseph Kennedy's indirect impact on the life of Aristotle Onassis. After leaving the SEC, and before going to London as our Ambassador, the senior Kennedy served as head of the Maritime Commission. In that capacity he instituted reforms that led, indirectly, to the indictment of Mr. Onassis for the illegal purchase of wartime surplus ships. The law that nailed Onassis was originally suggested by Kennedy. Mr. Onassis' $7,000,000 fine was the kind of sum Joseph P. Kennedy would have appreciated.

Jackie was the one who insisted that a physician be summoned on December 19, 1961, when Joseph Kennedy returned from the golf course to his Palm Beach home, where Jackie was staying, and said he didn't feel well. She helped him upstairs; the Ambassador said he would be O.K. and please don't call the doctor. Jackie disobeyed his order. Not long after that, it was announced that he had become partially paralyzed.

All the Kennedys and Jackie were together, once again, the day Joseph P. Kennedy was buried. It was probably for the last time.

Chapter Sixteen

JOHN & CAROLINE &
CHRISTINA &
ALEXANDER

D iscussing John Kennedy's family shortly after he was killed, the New York *Times* said: "After all, the Kennedys are as close as America will ever get to having its own royalty, and people's interest in the children is just not very likely to fade."

Unfortunately, *some* people's interest in John Kennedy's children is downright psychopathic, unbelievably vicious. Not long ago Jackie, with some understatement, said: "Things happen to them that do not necessarily happen to other children. Caroline was knocked down by a charge of photographers when I took her to Switzerland to try to teach her to ski. How do you explain that to a child? And the stares and the pointing!"

There was another, more brutal, incident involving Caroline. One All Saints' Day, when Jackie and the chil-

dren were coming out of church, Caroline lagged somewhat behind in the bustle at the exit. A strange, wretched,
sick woman leaped at her and shouted: "Your mother is a
wicked woman who has killed three people. And your
father is still alive."

Properly incensed by these events and, once again,
forced to think of the lunatics at large in this world, in
relationship to Caroline and John, Jackie said that she
didn't give a hoot what slanders were directed against
her, but why should the children be in jeopardy? When
she and the children became New Yorkers, she assailed the
Jackie-watchers, forever at her door, and was outraged
at the *Saturday Evening Post*, which had printed an
article billed on the cover as—"The National Sport of
Jackie Watching"—and illustrated it with a map titled:
"Jackie Kennedy's Manhattan."

"Why a map?" complained Jackie. "And a detailed dia-
gram showing just where the children are at various times
of the day? Why is it important to give our address, or the
name of the children's schools and times of classes? Why?"

No reasonable journalist could deny Jackie's right to
be infuriated by that piece in the *Post*, but the *Post* was
not the only offender. Even ten-year-old John Kennedy,
Jr.'s, agility at the gentlemanly sport of fisticuffs was a
subject for national attention. One magazine reported that
when John was in the third grade, the mother of one of
his classmates at New York's Collegiate School was
shocked when her son came home with a bloody nose.
"John Kennedy did it," the little boy reported. "I called
him 'John-John' and he socked me. But don't worry. I hit
him back."

If John is in the mood, there are the noses of some
very famous people's sons to work over at Collegiate,

which is 332-years-old, or 138 years older than the United States of America. There are in attendance, for example, boys sired by Leonard Bernstein, ballet dancer Jacques d'Amboise, whiskey magnate Edgar Bronfman, and actor Jason Robards, Jr.

The venerable day school has tried to do everything in its power to treat John Kennedy, Jr., as if he were just another pupil whose family can afford the stiff tuition, but it's not easy. Not every nine-year-old boy has a mother whose picture is always in the newspapers, and a step-father with a yacht longer than a Staten Island ferryboat. Not every nine-year-old boy is driven to school accompanied by a French governess and two pistol-packing Secret Servicemen, one a cigar-chomper called "Muggsy."

John, Jr., is probably not aware that when he was admitted to Collegiate, hundreds of New York parents used some pretty unflattering words to the effect that the Kennedys were once again throwing their weight around. The reason was that only one out of every forty boys whose family tries to enroll him in Collegiate is admitted. And so, as usual, the cry was "favoritism," a charge which the school denied.

On top of that, a newspaper reported that John had left his previous school, St. David's, because he was going to be held back and made to repeat the second grade, and his mother wouldn't have that. The newspaper said John, something less than a whiz kid academically, regarded homework as a bore to be avoided, and that he often whooped it up, racing through the corridors and detaching things, like fire extinquishers and notices on bulletin boards, as though he were a one-boy anti-Establishment riot.

The implication of all this was that the Collegiate

School had accepted a student who wasn't capable of shaping up to the regular rigid entrance examinations. But Carl Andrews, a Collegiate teacher, says that's "stuff and utter nonesense."

"Be assured," said Mr. Andrews, "that not even a Kennedy can get into Collegiate if he can't do the work. John was accepted because he is a very bright little boy. He received no special treatment. He enrolled and had to wait a year until we had a place for him."

John's doing fine at Collegiate, everybody says. And he's a Big Man on the Campus, which in this case is Central Park, because he can pass a football like a pint-sized Joe Namath and also scores more touchdowns than anyone else in his class. (That Olympic-style training camp called "The Compound" at Hyannis Port has its points.)

Escorted by Secret Servicemen, Caroline, now twelve, walks the six blocks from her home to her school, the Convent of the Sacred Heart, which occupies a gingerbread mansion at 91st Street and Fifth Avenue. Her classmates are the daughters of New York's elite, and on a rainy day the street in front of the school is jammed with Rolls-Royces and governesses and uniformed chauffeurs holding umbrellas over their charges.

The nuns who operate the Convent of the Sacred Heart rave about Caroline, and so do the parents of other students who know her. One said: "She's terrifically bright. She'd stand out in any group, even if she weren't Caroline Kennedy."

Caroline's report card is one long string of A's, but she is no nose-stuck-in-the-book grind. The playing fields of Hyannis Port have also left their mark on Caroline, and she's a formidable athlete. She sits a horse perfectly, and rides to hounds (in New Jersey and Maryland) with complete confidence and lack of concern for the scariest jumps. At volleyball and basketball she has the fierce Kennedy competitive spirit, and more than once, during basketball games, she has been warned that a proper young lady's elbow should *not* be violently poked into an opposing player's ribs.

One mother, who appeared somewhat honored by the whole thing, said: "During one basketball game Caroline Kennedy blocked my daughter so vigorously that the air came out of the child as if she were a punctured inner tube."

But while Caroline's prowess at studies and sports must please Jackie, the girl has another asset which, in the world she will live in, is vastly more important. Caroline Kennedy has the makings of a great beauty. She now looks more like her mother than her father, and her features are perfect. She wears her thick blond hair pulled straight back from her face and tied with a bow. Her eyes are bright blue, and when her face lights up and she laughs, every adult in the room feels dandy, like spring, fresh-cut roses, champagne.

Caroline Kennedy will be the world's most famous teenager and, with the blood that's in her, will probably try to top her mother, which is a staggering challenge. ("It's a shame she's not several years older," said a British aristocrat recently. "She would be just perfect for our Prince Charles.")

When Aristotle Onassis married Jacqueline Kennedy he said that he had no intention of trying to be a "father" to John and Caroline. He was too old to reach out and establish a parental rapport with children so young. And how could he dare try to "stand in" for John Fitzgerald Kennedy? It wouldn't look right, it wouldn't work. Mr.

Onassis showers the children with gifts; he is to John and Caroline a kind of year-round Kriss Kringle, what with the yacht and private aircraft and donkey rides on groovy Greek islands. You name it, he will be happy to provide it.

Caroline and John don't see their stepfather very often, but they never saw their own father very often, either. By the time Caroline was born John Kennedy was already in full pursuit of his political ambitions, forever on the move, speaking in different parts of the country several times a week, seldom home for dinner. There almost never was an evening when he and Jackie would sit down with the children for a family-style meal.

No one has ever questioned Jackie's devotion to Caroline and John, but there has always been on hand a governess, a "substitute mother." In the White House it was the austere Englishwoman, Maude Shaw; now it is a Swiss girl, who is teaching the children conversational French.

Jackie simply could never find a lot of time to give to the children. During the White House years Caroline and John were led into Mrs. Kennedy's sitting room—if she was not otherwise engaged—before their bedtime and Jackie would read them a story. Well, one never expected Jackie, the way she herself was raised, to go around playing hopscotch with Caroline and mixing formulas and changing John's diapers. A long time ago Jackie made it very clear this was not to be her thing. When she graduated from Miss Porter's, her profile in the gaggy yearbook said that Jackie's ambition was: "Not to be a housewife."

It is not surprising that, since the Kennedys produce children practically on an assembly line, whenever the clan convenes the number of governesses and other domestics on hand is sufficient to start a third party. After spending a weekend as a guest at Hyannis Port, a Bostonian said: "The social rating at the compound is on three levels. First, the family. Then the private secretaries and governesses—there seems to be a small army of them. Then the ordinary domestics—house servants, chauffeurs, gardeners, porters, etcetera."

Since Jackie married Mr. Onassis, Caroline and John are seeing even less of their mother than they did in the White House. Jackie makes it her business to spend some weeks in New York during the school year, but she spends more weeks in Greece, London, Paris, or in the Caribbean. Caroline and John, who are already jet setters, fly to Europe for Christmas. They celebrated the first Christmas that Jackie was Mrs. Onassis aboard the *Christina*, which had two trees on deck, one forward and one aft. And they celebrated last Christmas with Jackie at Lee Radziwill's country home in England.

During the summer Caroline and John are passed from hand to hand like hot dogs being passed along a row of seats at a baseball game. They spend a short while with Jackie and Ari in Greece. Then they visit their maternal grandmother, Mrs. Hugh Auchincloss, at her "gentleman's" farm, Hammersmith, in Newport. Then they're off to be supervised by Rose Kennedy at Hyannis Port. (For a couple of teen-agers, Caroline and John have little reason ever to feel cooped up.)

There's a story in circulation about jet-set children that concerns a friend of Jackie and Ari's. After returning from a leisurely global cruise aboard her yacht recently, she seemed troubled and told her friends: "I *must* find more time to spend with the children. When I walked into the apartment the other afternoon Lois, she's the six-year-old, didn't seem to recognize me, and she started to cry."

Even when Caroline and John go to Greece, they're parked with nanny in a separate, distant suite. This "separate but equal" treatment of jet-set children is the basis of a story told about the late Eugenie Niarchos, before she divorced Stavros. Eugenie was holidaying on the Riviera, and one evening she telephoned her husband, who was at their home in London.

"Stavros, how are the children?" Eugenie asked.

"The children?" Mr. Niarchos replied, puzzled. "But darling—they're with you!"

A friend close to the Kennedy family's financial office in New York's Pan Am Building says that the cost of maintaining John and Caroline—their allowances, clothes, tuition, governesses, and general upkeep—comes to $30,000 a year. That, of course, will skyrocket as they grow up and show, as one might expect, an interest in making the international scene on their own.

Aristotle Onassis' children, Alexander, twenty-one, and Christina, nineteen, were raised in an even more baronial atmosphere than the Kennedys, with servants always within calling distance to fetch things and pick things up. Christina didn't dress herself until she was well into her teens.

The terrible moment in their lives came on the day in 1960 when they were told that their father and their mother, Tina Livanos, had decided on divorce. Alexander went into a tantrum, throwing things and biting, and Christina cried for days. They were in total, united opposition to the divorce and they have always hoped that, somehow, their parents would be reunited.

Alexander and Christina were again shattered when their mother told them, several years after splitting with Ari, that she was going to marry the Marquess of Blandford, a nice enough aristocrat, with a certain percentage of royal blood, but very bland compared to the exuberant Ari. Friends in London recall that the Onassis children actually filibustered against the proposed marriage, hoping to stall it long enough for their mother to change her mind. The whole thing became messy, and there were leaks to the press. An expected announcement from Blenheim Palace, the Marquess's ancestral home (where Winston Churchill was born), was not forthcoming, and Tina and her fiancé slipped out of London and were married, practically incognito, in Paris.

Having lost that struggle, Alexander and Christina were then faced with a new ordeal: Their father entered into his long association with Maria Callas, and the children were determined that this business not be legalized at the altar. They made faces behind Callas' back, and on the yacht they splashed her with water and in every way treated her like an unwanted guest. One day they piled on her in the swimming pool with such force that the poor diva thought she was going to drown. She put an end to that by yanking Christina's hair so hard the girl screamed, and by ramming her knee into an area of Alexander's anatomy that is protected by the Marquess of Queensberry's rules.

Alexander and Christina were just as hostile and sullen about Ari's marriage to Jacqueline Kennedy. After reluctantly attending the Onassis-Kennedy nuptials on Skorpios, Alexander told reporters in Paris: "I didn't need a stepmother, but my father needed a wife."

When Alexander and Chistina are together with their stepfather or stepmother, they tolerate the Marquess and Jackie, but the climate is as cozy as Antarctica. Alexander, particularly, has a sharp tongue, which is honed when he is drinking, and on more than one occasion he has directed it at Jackie. During a dinner party at Maxim's, according to one of the guests, Alexander was being gently ribbed about one of his current girl friends, a show girl of most humble origin. Turning to his stepmother, Alexander said: "Jackie, *you* certainly don't think there's anything wrong in a girl marrying for money, do you?"

Last winter Jackie told an old chum: "I really am very fond of Alexander—when Ari and I are on the high seas and Alex is on the other side of the world."

Some catty jet setters told writer Liz Smith, who chronicles the Beautiful People, that Alexander and Christina fought tooth and nail against their father's marrying Jackie for another reason, a selfish one—they were afraid it would cost them a few hundred million dollars, in case Jackie and Ari get divorced, or when their father dies. "One close friend," wrote Miss Smith, "said that both Alexander and Christina consider their new mother to be a businesswoman in her marital affairs."

It is understood that every time Alexander and Christina read that their stepmother has bought herself another mink, or several, they moan and groan. They feel it's just so much money out of their pocketbooks. Not that the poor dears will ever have to scrounge a meal!

Christina and Alexander are joint beneficiaries of a trust fund valued at $40,000,000. Since he married Jackie, Mr. Onassis has contributed another $1,000,000 to the fund.

Alexander Onassis, who these days gets a $100,000 annual allowance, has been called an "apprentice playboy." At the advanced age of 15, he gave a jumping party in a Riviera nightclub during which he and his guests acted like militant students rampaging a dean's office. They tossed around plates and overturned champagne buckets and agitated the management into calling the *flics*. Through the years Daddy O has picked up numerous fat tabs for such damages.

For some time Alexander whizzed around Monte Carlo in a specially built electric car, then he acquired a souped-up, red Ferrari—and paid enough traffic fines to refurbish Princess Grace's palace.

One time Ari, concerned that Alexander was cutting up too much, called him into his office on the *Christina* for a father-to-son chat. He urged his son to take life more seriously, then pointed to the valuable paintings and rich fixtures and said: "I had to work for all this, I didn't start with it."

Alexander replied matter-of-factly: "But *I* did."

Alexander and Christina are, as much as any of the other super-rich siblings around, typical children of the jet set. In their various sumptuous homes they've seen the great, beautiful, wise, evil, and the very, very rich come to flatter, impress, or con their father, who is not exactly an easy mark. Nothing has ever been denied them; there has been little restraint. If they are spoiled and arrogant, as some people say, you can't blame them. Both have inherited Ari's taste for the purchasable pleasures.

Alexander pursues women with such intensity that one of his fellow playboys has said: "Alex changes girl friends as often as he changes shirts." Although nothing breathing and female has been known to escape his attention, he has always had a particular hankering for ladies who are some years his senior. At an astonishingly early age, according to a reliable source, one of his governesses, a comely Scot, turned in her resignation to Mr. Onassis with the bitter comment that, while she had no quarrel with her wages, she had no intention of co-operating with his son's demands to convert the nursery into a workshop course in sex education. Since he's been eighteen Alexander has been squiring older women. One was the European movie actress Patricia Viterbo, another was Odile Rubirosa, the widow of the frolicsome Dominican, Porfirio Rubirosa,

At the time this book was committed to the printer, Alexander had astounded the jet set by reducing, at least on the surface, his number of steady girl friends to one, thirty-eight-year-old Baroness Fiona Thyssen-Bornemisza, and he was quite openly talking about making her his bride.

This was not a development in any way pleasing to his father, for besides being seventeen years his son's senior, the Baroness is a divorcée with two children. Ari, would, like any doting parent, much prefer his son to take to the altar a female in his own age bracket, someone who could surely bear children and continue the Onassis Empire. It was reported that when Mr. Onassis tossed a twenty-first birthday party for Alexander in May, 1969, the boy pointed to a bottle of Scotch on the table near his father and asked: "Say, Dad, do you mind if I take some whiskey?" Ari snapped: "Take anything you want— only *don't* take Fiona."

The Baroness Thyssen-Bornemisza is not a member of one of those hyphenated, down-at-the-heels European families out to ensnare the heir to a fat fortune by employing the ancient secrets of her sex. She is neither royal in blood nor poor in purse. Her father, although himself well hyphenated, is a mere seagoing servant of the British Crown, Rear Admiral Keith McNeil Campbell-Walter.

In her teens the Baroness cut three parts off her name and, as Fiona Campbell, set out to be a model. She had the proper perfect face, proper brunette hair, proper teeth, proper bones, proper legs, and the proper manners, and she was quickly associated with the proper English *couturier*, the House of Hartnell. Soon she was an exciting new ornament of the Mayfair division of the jet set, and for a while she was ardently pursued by the Earl of Dalkeith, who is kind of a loser—the Earl also bid for, and failed to win, the hand of Princess Margaret. In 1955, when Alexander Onassis was seven, Fiona Campbell married Baron Thyssen-Bornemisza, a man of old, if somewhat controversial, money. His money comes from his family's interest in the giant German Krupp Works, which armed Germany in two world wars.

After a somewhat rocky nine-year marriage, the Thyssen-Bornemiszas were divorced, and the Baron settled on his lady a sum that has been reported, somewhat vaguely, to be in the neighborhood of several million dollars. At the time she split with the Baron, Fiona sighed: "Luxury and riches do not make for conjugal happiness." Poor is better?

The Alexander-Fiona romance gave the Jackie-watchers something new to chew over. They assumed that Jackie, along with her husband, regards the affair with dismay, because, for one thing, the Baroness, who might become her stepson's wife, is only three years younger than she is.

Alexander, as hard-nosed as his father, is not likely to bend too easily before the parental storm. And, if the marriage does come off, it will be nice, in a way, for Caroline and John Kennedy, when they visit Skorpios or the *Christina*. They'll have some playmates almost their own age; the Thyssen-Bornemisza children, Francesca and Lorne, are eleven and seven.

Alexander, who is active in his father's various enterprises, jets around Europe most of the time, but Christina is a New Yorker by choice. She has her own $2,500-a-month apartment in the Hotel Pierre on Fifth Avenue, and enough credit cards in her purse to buy Brazil. Since Christina is more of a homebody, her annual allowance is only $75,000.

Christina's steady beau is more to Ari and Jackie's taste. He is John Goulandris, twenty-two-year-old scion of the Greek shipping clan that also counts its blessings in the hundreds of millions of dollars. If Christina and John eventually do get married, it will be like the Chase Manhattan Bank merging with First National City.

One thing's for sure—neither the Onassis children nor the children of John Fitzgerald Kennedy face a bleak economic future. Very careful in the selection of their parents, each one was born "retired," if they so desired.

Jackie says her children can stay "retired" and do anything they want with their lives, as long as it's not downright kookie and unhealthy, and she won't stand in their way, with one exception. Even though there's already been some talk about nominating John for the Presidency in the late '90's, when he'll be eligible for the first time, Jackie hopes he will stay out of politics. Enough is enough!

Certainly Caroline and John, simply by being Kennedys, are very rich citizens, and their trust funds will grow yet richer with time. But Jackie's children, and, for that matter, all the children of the Kennedy clan, will probably never be in the same money class with Jacqueline Onassis. For it seems inevitable that Jackie will become "The Richest Woman in the World."

Aristotle Onassis is now in his sixties, and Jackie is almost a quarter of a century younger. So it is reasonable to expect that someday she will inherit a sum almost too mighty to comprehend. Since his children and his relatives are already well taken care of by trust funds and shares in the business, the vast bulk of Mr. Onassis' fortune—something like a billion dollars—will probably go to Jacqueline Bouvier Kennedy Onassis.

Even if Jackie only inherits one half that much, she'll be way above any other American or foreign woman of means. The richest woman in the United States has been Mrs. Mellon Bruce, whose holdings are said to be in the neighborhood of $400,000,000. Then there's Mrs. Frederick Guest, with only $300,000,000, and Mrs. Edsel Ford with $150,000,000. Doris Duke has only $110,000,-000, and Barbara Hutton's holdings are under $100,000,000 —enough, surely, but not as much as Jackie will have. Jackie will have hundreds of millions of dollars more than all the Kennedys put together. They've only got $300,000,000 to $400,000,000, and since Joseph P. Kennedy died no one in the family has demonstrated the same magic dollar-multiplying touch.

What a string of titles Jackie has had in her remarkable lifetime! First she was Debutante of the Year. Then she was First Lady of the United States. Now she is Wife of the Richest Man on Earth. And in the misty tomorrow she will be The Richest Woman in the World.

It is understandable that most of us look upon such bediamonded people as unreal—as either blessed with glamour and excitement or as being irrelevant or useless or even malevolent. They seen totally remote, in the way they live and in the values they live by, from the majority of mankind. The very rich, it has been said, are different

from you and me—they have more money. But no couple
—however rich—is so different that, whey they are newly
wed, one does not wish them a full and happy life together.

It seems likely Jackie and Ari have found it.

BIBLIOGRAPY

In addition to the leg work on my part, I read just about everything that has been written in every major language on the first year of Jackie and Ari's marriage. Even at this early stage, there had been more written about them than was written about the entire Children's Crusade! It is, thus, impossible for me to enumerate all the printed sources that have been of help in the writing of this book. Below are some of the most important publications that were valuable. I should also add every major newspaper magazine, and wire service in the world.

Adler, Bill. *The Kennedy Wit*. New York: The Citadel Press, 1964.

Baldridge, Letitia. *Of Diamonds and Diplomats*. Boston: Houghton-Mifflin Co., 1969.

Beebe, Lucius. *Big Spenders*. New York: Doubleday & Co., 1966.

Bishop, Jim. *A Day in the Life of President Kennedy*. New York: Random House, 1964.

Carpozi, George, Jr. *The Hidden Side of Jacqueline Kennedy*. New York: Lancer, 1968.

Carpozi, George, Jr. *Jackie and Ari*. New York: Lancer, 1968.

Damore, Lee. *The Cape Cod Years of John Fitzgerald Kennedy*. New York: Prentice-Hall, 1967.

de Toledano, Ralph. *R. F. K.—The Man Who Would Be President*. New York: G. P. Putnam's Sons, 1967.

Frischauer, Willi. *Onassis*. New York: Meredith Press, 1968.

Galbraith, John Kenneth. *Ambassador's Journal*. Boston: Houghton-Mifflin Co., 1969.

Gallagher, Mary B. *My Life with Jacqueline Kennedy*. New York: David McKay Co., 1969.

Getty, J. Paul. *How to Be Rich*. New York: Trident Press, 1966.

Joeston, Joachin, *Onassis*. London: Abelard-Schuman, 1963.

239

240   *Bibliography*

Lincoln, Evelyn. *My Twelve Years with John F. Kennedy.* New York: David McKay Co., 1964.

Lundberg, Ferdinand. *The Rich and the Super-rich.* New York: Lyle Stuart, 1968.

Shaw, Maud. *White House Nannie.* New York: New American Library, 1966.

Thayer, Mary Van Rensselaer. *Jacqueline Bouvier Kennedy.* Doubleday & Co., 1961.

Whalen, Richard. *The Founding Father.* New York: New American Library, 1964.

Zierod, Norman, *Garbo.* New York: Stein and Day, 1969.

Zotos, Stephanos. *The Greeks.* New York: Funk & Wagnalls, 1969.

ABOUT THE AUTHOR

FRED SPARKS has been bylined by the London *Daily Mail* as "one of the greatest reporters in America." *Newsweek* described him as "one of the last of the journeymen journalists". A living legend in journalism, Mr. Sparks's work is known from New York to Tokyo and from New Delhi to Baghdad. He was awarded the Pulitzer Prize for International Reporting in 1951. Mr. Sparks first met Aristotle Onassis in Athens as a result of his friendship with Queen Frederika. Since Mr. Onassis married Jackie Kennedy, Sparks has watched the couple as carefully as the CIA watches the Kremlin—and this book is the result.